# Boys Don't Cry; MEN DO

Alberto Minzer, A.C.S.W.,L.C.S.W.,C.A.D.C.

Edited by
Larry E. Clary

Bloomington, IN  Milton Keynes, UK

authorHOUSE™

AuthorHouse™
1663 Liberty Drive, Suite 200
Bloomington, IN 47403
www.authorhouse.com
Phone: 1-800-839-8640

AuthorHouse™ UK Ltd.
500 Avebury Boulevard
Central Milton Keynes, MK9 2BE
www.authorhouse.co.uk
Phone: 08001974150

First published by AuthorHouse 5/15/2006

ISBN: 1-4259-2620-7 (sc)

Library of Congress Control Number: 2006903132

Printed in the United States of America
Bloomington, Indiana

This book is printed on acid-free paper.

# Contents

# Acknowledgements

It would not have been possible for me to do this writing without those individuals who contributed in shaping my ideas for this book. I also want to thank those individuals who believed in and supported my work and encouraged me to complete this writing. The power of belief, one of the greatest gifts a human being can give another, was given freely to me. No words of gratitude can express my thankfulness to these individuals. Lastly, to those who I did not acknowledge by name, thank you. You know who you are.

I'd like to thank Jay Lewis for his consistent inquiry about my writings, always believing in me and what I had to say, as well as providing constructive feedback about my ideas. A lifetime friend I will never forget.

I also want to thank the following people for their input and support: Keith Endo, Dave Lambert, Barry Newman, Doug Moran, Dr. Charles Falk, and Dr. Richard Markin. I'd also like to thank Jim Werwath, Scott Thompson, Christopher R. Conty, Paul Patterson, Tom Johnston, and Harvey Rabichow, for contributing additional resources that men will draw on, in their path toward healing.

My heart-felt thanks go to Dr. John Everingham, a teacher, writer, mentor, and elder, who blessed my work and endorsed my manuscript. He encouraged and empowered my views on the subject. His feedback and input helped me solidify the convictions I already had, about the issues and the struggles men face in their healing journey.

I want to thank Reid Baer for his critical review and endorsement of my manuscript. His support gave me the confidence that I was on the right track to finish this project.

A special thanks to a colleague and my first editor, Lenore D. Smith. She took my first manuscript draft when I began giving birth to this book, and gave me invaluable support and feedback. In the early stages of my manuscript her belief in my work encouraged me to build on my ideas and elaborate on my chapters. Other colleagues I would like to thank for their support are Michelle McCullough and Jane Rooney. Also Freddi Krell, a wonderful woman, an old wise soul, for her big heart and her loving ways of giving to others, as she gave to me, unconditionally, in my daily work. Thank you, Freddi, for just being you; you've made a difference in my life.

This book would not have been completed without the help of Larry Clary, the editor that came into my life at the right time, convincing me again that there's synchronicity in the universe; and the universe brought us together to bring life to this book, somehow providing additional structure, form, and shape to my ideas, and giving them the voice I wanted the reader to hear. Many hours were spent together bouncing ideas, sharing our lives, and blending my convictions with his skills to bring my ideas into a readable form. His gift of clarity made my ideas come to life. My conviction that mature men seek support and ask for help became alive throughout our working relationship, which has been filled with the lessons learned in collaborative work, the flow of ideas, the extreme patience, the attentive listening, and the depth of honesty that's possible in transformational men's work. He brought me lessons learned in this collaborative work, the flow of ideas, always patient, always attentive, and honest in the work. His own integrity taught me to see more levels of reality than my own. I will never forget how we finished the editing of our last chapter, "The Blessing." It was 2:00 in the morning, and we were still sitting on the front balcony of his beautiful old house on a summer night, and still talking and making changes and feeling proud that we could touch the lives of other men. And then we looked at each other and said "we're done." We not only knew it, we felt it. How sweet this moment was, after all the work. I'm thankful for the journey he took with me.

I'd also like to thank my two daughters, whose precious lives have given me as much as I've given them. Their lives intertwining with mine, never ever letting me forget what's most important. In all of this, there is one person who sits next to me, and who has known me more than any other, my loving wife. With her love, belief in me, critical support, relentless desire to seek my ultimate truth as well as her own, and desire to share her life with me, she has helped me reach this point in my life. Thank you for everything. My unconsciousness knew what I didn't know consciously a long time ago; she's always been the one. My family continues to teach me the meaning of love, and constantly challenges me to be authentic.

I am truly blessed in my life and humbly say thank you to you all. May these kernels of truth take you further on your journey of bountiful and limitless potential.

Blessings,
Alberto Minzer, MSW, LCSW, CADC

# Foreword

I've chosen to share my struggle to illuminate what many men go through. I also write from a professional perspective, as a psychotherapist who has spent 22 years in practice. It would not have been possible for me to write this book without the clients I have worked with, who have entrusted their lives with me by sharing their stories. Through their life stories, the pain they expressed, the fears, the longings, they revealed their wounded hearts. It was in sacred moments like these that I gradually began to understand the significance of being emotionally alive. It was by their deep sharing that the authentic self began to take root firmly. It was their inner boy inside. So often, the inner boy was still there, waiting for someone to pay attention to him. It was that little boy who for some reason didn't think he was good enough, despite his trophies or good grades. The boy never really believed in himself. He didn't believe in himself, because he didn't have the experience of knowing that anyone else really believed in him. I have met many men who still carry the little boy inside, who feels unwanted, betrayed, unloved and abandoned. Physically, these little boys did grow up. As men, many have become quite successful by society's standards. Yet, the yearning for love was still there. Emotionally, the little boys had not grown into healthy, fulfilled men.

This book is for men and about men, but can be read by women that want to get a better understanding of how most men struggle in their own silent ways. Even though many don't appear to be, most men I have worked with in my practice have a great deal of difficulty being authentic, "being themselves." This book may help clarify what is behind the mask that so many men wear, or perhaps help you understand yourself or someone whom you care deeply about.

This book was also written for all who love these men, who know they can be much healthier, happier men than they already are. These writings will clarify how men are taught to live in ways that do not ultimately serve them or others. It is also about how to begin healing by living in authenticity-- by paying attention to the ways and the needs of the grown man's heart.

As you read this book, you may choose to read entire chapters more than once. You might return to some sections over and over, and find new meaning each time. Don't be in a hurry to finish, as though your growth will be complete when you've finished the last page. It won't be complete, because personal growth takes time. So read it slowly. Give yourself the time to absorb the book's meaning for you and for the people you care about.

Boys don't cry; men do.

Alberto Minzer, MSW, LCSW, CADC
Chicago, August, 2005

### Tired Of Speaking Sweetly

*Love wants to reach out and manhandle us,*
*Break all our teacup talk of God.*
*If you had the courage and*
*Could give the Beloved His choice, some nights,*
*He would just drag you around the room*
*By your hair,*
*Ripping from your grip all those toys in the world*
*That bring you no joy.*

*Love sometimes gets tired of speaking sweetly*
*And wants to rip to shreds*
*All your erroneous notions of truth*
*That make you fight within yourself, dear one,*
*And with others,*
*Causing the world to weep*
*On too many fine days.*
*God wants to manhandle us,*
*Lock us inside of a tiny room with Himself*
*And practice His dropkick.*
*The Beloved sometimes wants*
*To do us a great favor:*
*Hold us upside down*
*And Shake all the nonsense out.*
*But when we hear*
*He is in a "playful drunken mood"*
*Most everyone I know*
*Quickly packs their bags and hightails it*
*Out of town.*

**Hafiz**
**14ᵗʰ Century Poet**

# Chapter 1
# My View of the World

I believe my life is like yours. Critical choices influence each of us, and shape our lives. Each life can be described as a set of choices, followed by the results of those choices. As we grow through childhood and into adulthood and maturity, each of us develops our own understanding of personal responsibility for the consequences of our choices.

Children need the protection and care of their parents. They have no control (and no true influence) over choices that are made. As children, we don't have the tools and awareness to talk about what matters to us. We don't even have the recognition or understanding of happiness, or words to describe it.

Because children are powerless over the choices made for them, they experience the consequences of these choices without being responsible for the events that follow the choices. This is a part of the true innocence of the young. And as innocence is replaced by experience, each of us gains maturity, and can be expected to gain responsibility for our choices.

In my lifetime of witnessing my own growth and the growth of others, I've learned to see the difference between growing and becoming mature. Unlike children, grown men can develop the tools and the awareness to know what matters in their lives. Grown men often do have the words to ask for what matters most to them.

1

Even so, many men fail to grow beyond that understanding, to create the happiness that they crave. Men who live their lives with the ability to create their own joy have reached a higher level of understanding, where each man accepts that he has the full responsibility for his own happiness, and takes the steps to make things happen in his life. In my view of the world, this understanding identifies the truly mature man, who can take action to bring joy into his life, and into the lives of others. This understanding of maturity is the key to finding the happiness that I want for me, and that I also want for you.

Each of us has a story to tell, of choices and experiences and the lessons learned from experiences, in each person's process of growth. I noticed in my own story that I gained more "understanding" from some experiences than from others; and I realize they were more significant to me because they brought me a big emotional connection to that event, whether it was a good or bad experience. All of a sudden, something just became incredibly clear, like I'd known it all my life! The more clear and memorable the experience, the greater the meaning it has had.

Maybe you've also experienced these kernel moments in your life, when a new interpretation of "how things work" has created or altered your view of the world. I interpret my experiences so that I can understand or explain the patterns in how the world works, based on the lessons that my experiences have taught me. I know men who lived a life-affirming childhood, whose beliefs about themselves and the world reflect that early experience, in a life-affirming and positive view of the world. I also know men whose childhood experiences included significant trauma, who view the world as a dangerous place where things can go terribly wrong, for no reason at all.

These men observe the same world; and in interpreting their memorable experiences, they "learn different lessons." One man might be confident and trusting and hopeful in all his relationships with others, while another man might have self doubt and lack the confidence that he will ever find happiness. Each man brings his view of the world into his adulthood, and it can become a self-fulfilling prophecy.

A man who believes he'll never find happiness is unlikely to recognize it (or trust that it will continue), even if he does experience it. As a man grows, he begins to rely on the lessons he has learned as a basis for understanding each of his new experiences, interpreting each event so that it's consistent with the interpretation of previous events. So, in adulthood, we begin to live out our childhood beliefs about how the world works and how it doesn't work. If a man begins to ignore the new lessons of his experience, he can only see the world as he has always seen it, and he stops maturing. At this moment, further growth is halted. He sees his world as he expects it to be, rather than how it actually is.

On the other hand, the man who stays open to the new lessons in his experience can continue to change, and can find new ways to achieve happiness.

So, how would you tell your own life story, to the person you trust most in the whole world?

To tell your story, you'll need to slow down now. Take a deep, slow breath, and close your eyes as you think about you as a child. Think about the possibility that this moment in your life could be a turning point. Did you ever feel as though something was missing, and you couldn't identify it? As though something was wrong with you, but you can't pinpoint what it is? Have you ever felt like everything you ever did was "wrong" somehow—that you always felt responsible for everything that went wrong, when you were a child? Do you have an unclear memory of faint voices, somehow telling you that you'll never be the man you want to be? That you're a failure?

We can't even count the number of ways in which you might have been abused, even by the people who loved you most, in their own ways. The pain of moments like these is part of what makes them memorable. These are just some of the ways that you may start remembering the story of your life.

You might also remember lessons that filled you with hope. Or your story might be like a heavy weight, from all the disappointments and sadness, and all the lessons that told you that your life would never be touched by joy. Take the time to review your story, for the lessons that you can learn again, maybe even in a new way. Even if your growth has stopped, realize that you can restart it. It all starts with a choice: choices, consequences, and then responsibility. It's just a choice.

When was the last time something happened, that changed your view of the world? If you're still willing to revise your view of the world, you can still create happiness in your life. You can change your view of the world. And you can change your life by accepting that you are the only person who is responsible for your happiness.

# Chapter 2
# My Story

I must go back where it all began. I lived in South America for the first 10 years of my life. I was born in Uruguay in the capital, Montevideo. Montevideo means "I see a mountain." One of my favorite excursions when I was a small child was to go to the mountaintop called El Cerro. From there I could see the whole city.

As a child, I woke up to the sounds of roosters crowing; the sounds of drying clothes as the wind blew them crispy dry on rooftops. I heard the sounds of the milkman's cart with horse and buggy as though it were Christmas. Each horse wore bells around its neck. I knew when they were close by. Best of all, my nostrils woke up filled with the smell of our neighbors' cooking. Once in a while, a loud screeching call from the man who sharpened kitchen knives and scissors would roll by. He would walk with his giant circular-stone-wheel cart in the middle of the street. The place I lived called me to wake up and face my day.

The women in the neighborhood started the day by sweeping the sidewalks, scrubbing as though the outside were parts of their homes. I knew everyone and everyone knew me.

Each Friday the outdoor market opened and it was the place to go. Only a block away from my home, we could buy everything we needed for the entire week. We had our favorite vendors. We were expected to bargain, and then walk away and come back for the sale. My grandmother was so good at this game that I would become embarrassed by how she would argue with vendors, and cuss them, and come back, buying their goods in the end.

My mother was a homemaker and my father was a salesman. My father would come home for lunch, and lunch would be ready for all of us. I would nap in the afternoon and wake up to a late snack of French bread with butter, sprinkled with sugar. Sometimes my grandmother would also shred carrots and sprinkle the sugar. I was never hungry. All my physical needs were met, yet I had a deeper craving that no one ever touched or helped me satisfy.

My grandparents emigrated from Poland prior to Nazi Germany in the early 1930's. All their family members who stayed behind were killed. They were among the few who took a ship, not knowing their destination. They spoke no Spanish. My grandmother once told me that she needed oil for frying, and she couldn't communicate to the vendor that she wanted oil.

My grandfather learned a trade and became a shoemaker. I always had good leather soles. My grandparents lived below us, in the two flat we shared with them. My parents, my twin brother and younger brother and I lived upstairs. I would spend hours on our front balcony, just sitting mostly with my grandfather, who liked to sit next to me without any words spoken. We would just sit and let time pass us by. At night everything quieted down, and the stars came out. I often went to the roof by myself, to watch the stillness of the night and wonder.

Even though I came from a community in which there was always someone around, I always felt alone inside. I came to know and embrace this aloneness, and to understand that it was the part of me. As a man, I know that this drove me to be what I am now. I never understood it consciously, but I knew that I was safest when I was alone. No one bothered me when I was alone. The adults in my life always told me what they wanted from me, and I always came short on delivering.

It was painful growing up Jewish. We were the only Jewish family in the predominantly Hispanic Catholic community. Almost every time there was a quarrel with my peers, they let me know I was a Jew, and not like them. I was ashamed, because I felt different inside. I knew I was not like my peers. I always felt a sense of distance. And when I fought with my friends on the block, sooner of later the anti-Semitic remarks started: "You miserable Jew, you people killed Jesus Christ."

As a child, I sought the approval of adults around me. I wanted to be like them. I would sneak inside the circle of adults, sitting around the dining room table or somewhere else in the house, talking amongst themselves. I wanted to know what they were talking about. Whatever it was, I wanted to know. To me playing hide and sneak, and marbles and war games were child's play. For some unknown reason, I believed the adults were having more fun. It must have been very important for adults to get together and talk. Boys didn't do that. I felt compelled to be around talking adults, because I didn't want to miss out on hearing what was so important.

Of course, this was a circle for adults only. Often I was told to leave. This generated even more curiosity for me, being so secretive. This was an exclusive club, which I could not wait to grow up and join. I thought this was a circle of the privileged. I know now that it was not that I craved to be an adult, but rather, I didn't want to be a child. I wanted to grow up fast and leave my childhood behind. Being a child was too painful; becoming an adult meant being pain free.

I had never flown on a plane until I came to Chicago at 10 years of age. All I could think about was that I wanted to fly on a plane. I remember saying goodbye to family and friends like it was no big deal. I was already unconscious and detached from my feelings. All I wanted to do was get on that plane and fly. I also thought about wanting to play in the snow, not knowing what snow would feel like in my hands. I think about that event now and this was a critical period in my life. All that I knew about, the life as I have known it to be, would change in less than 24 hours. The familiar would be no more. I would no longer speak my language but would need to speak a language that I did not know. My safety net was gone forever. The sights, sounds, smell, and places I had known all my life would become a memory. All that would be hidden, and only in reflection would I visit it again.

I remember my first school experience here. I felt so out of place. I didn't belong here. I wore different clothes than the rest of the kids. I spoke no English. The halls of the school appeared darker than I was accustomed to. I felt like I was in jail. In recovery there is a term they call "white knuckles," which means barely surviving day to day by the skin of your teeth. That is what it felt like, for the first five months of being in Chicago.

Of course, not fitting in, I became an easy target to be ridiculed and made fun of. Children at this age can be so cruel. This is the time for everyone when affiliation to a peer group is essential for survival. I had no peer group. I was on my own.

I remember that during a recess hour, I became the target of a prank, and it required several kids to pull it off. I was outside minding my own business as a kid pushes me backward, while another one was kneeling behind me. I fell back to the snowy ground, and one of them proceeded to took off my shoes. I heard them laugh; and in total humiliation I began walking home in my socks, which was three to four blocks, in the winter. My mother was home at that time and I was crying. She could not believe what had happened. Determined to bring some justice to this surreal event, my mother and I went back to school, to the principal's office. My mother wasn't able to speak English; but fortunately, the principal understood some Yiddish, an old Jewish dialect. The principal, my mother, and I went back to the classroom, and they spoke to the teacher. I couldn't understand what was being said; but all I got from this confrontation is that I started this, and it was my fault. Once again, I was humiliated and shamed.

I had no clue what people were talking about, for these first five months in school. I felt totally inadequate, and stupid. I had good grades in South America and I was a good student. As a result of the difficulties I was having, I had to retake the fifth grade. Yet I learned the language rather quickly. It was a matter of survival.

11

Also I remember being ten years old, standing on a corner as a patrol boy for my school, when the thought came to me that I wanted to become a psychotherapist. I had no reference to this profession, but I knew that it required listening to people's problems. Of course, this was a projection of the need for help that I felt. I didn't realize how disconnected I was at the time, but I know now that I was probably struggling already with depression.

My parents, not being psychologically inclined, felt worried about me and began taking me to doctors. Having a child with psychological problems was a stigma to them and to the majority of individuals from my parents' generation. Of course there was nothing wrong medically, and at that time I don't recall any doctor telling them I needed psychological help. My parents must have known something was wrong, without knowing what it was.

Before finishing the eighth grade, my parents decided to return to Uruguay. My father worked very hard in a factory in the States, and my mother began working for the first time in her life as a manicurist. The life they once had was gone. This was work, hard work. Neither of them seemed happy.

I was glad to go home to Uruguay. My parents bought everything except furniture to bring back. My father placed all these items in large wooden containers and shipped them to South America. When we arrived a month later, we found out most of the items had been stolen. My father was furious and disappointed. He wanted to open up a gas station in Uruguay. When we arrived, the economy was terrible, and my father saw no chance of making a profit. We stayed less than a year, before returning to Chicago.

I absolutely didn't want to come back to the States. I felt I was back home in Uruguay, but this was shorted lived. I was certainly still too young to take care of myself, and I still needed my parents.

By my late teens I was clearly fighting against depression. The movie *Harold and Maude* had a great impact on me, with its story about an older woman and a younger man who developed a relationship and fell in love. They both lived the life they wanted, regardless of the norm. When they were separated by Maude's death, through suicide, Harold continued to live the brave life that they had together. They gave me the courage to change my life; and after seeing that movie I was ready. I felt I needed to find myself, and I lived abroad for seven months of adventure.

Yet I couldn't help myself with the high level of anxiety and feelings of depression I still felt. I remember I became a volunteer in a plantation field in Israel. Inside this plantation one day, I had a panic attack and felt like I was going crazy. I was in a jungle, and I felt like I couldn't find my way back. I started running, finally locating the crew, and telling no one how scared and crazy and needy I had felt. A short time later, my girlfriend broke up with me, telling me she was not able to handle a close relationship at this time in her life. That was a big loss in my life. My depression worsened, and I felt I needed to return home to my parents. I was glad to be "home" initially, but my elation was short lived. I felt lost. I didn't even know what I wanted to do in the course of a day. So I slept a lot—sleeping was a way to pass the day. I didn't want to feel the pain of my life. I was watching television one morning, feeling lots of despair, when I heard Leo Buscaglia for the first time, talking about the power of loving relationships. I was 21 years old, when I realized I needed help.

Going to a psychotherapist was a turning point in my life. Since that time, I've studied and practiced psychotherapy, and I've found many tools that have helped me learn about myself, and to grow emotionally. Each step along the way has brought me closer to being the authentic man that I am becoming, in every day of my life. The path was long, and at times it felt hopeless. Yet, mysteriously, I began to accept guidance from others. I trusted enough to know that this was a path I would not do alone, but with the help of others.

Even though I felt tortured by my depression as a very young man, I want to share with you here that every piece of my story was perfect, and everything happened for a reason. During my times when I felt lost, I found new opportunities that felt like an oasis.

All of my experiences have led me to this point, and I can see that even the most painful moments were essential in creating the life I have now. I love my life, and I'm truly happy. I know from the deepest part of me that you can also have what I feel now—hope, freedom, and joy.

# Chapter 3
# Our Early Days: Lessons We Teach Ourselves

Growing up, no adult ever told me what it really took to become a man. I didn't have good role models to help me with the little boy within, who wanted to be a man. For many years, I lived a lie. I discovered in adulthood that becoming the man I had dreamed about had a cost, which I was not aware of as a child. The cost is that I would have to look at the pain I was feeling, in order to give up the illusion that I wasn't feeling pain. No adult ever taught me, or even shared with me, this lesson in life. I had to discover this on my own, through my own soul- searching, with many twists and turns, in finally finding truths about myself.

Looking back now, it seems as though nobody understood me. Each of us needs teachers, mentors, guides, around us, despite the fact that there may have been men present in our lives. Those men who perhaps were your teachers were from the "old" world. The lessons you probably learned were to deny all those aspects of you that were not considered "macho;" you were taught to be stern, tough, self assured, independent, above feelings. You perhaps feared these men and their lessons. It may have been part of your initiation to kill off the little boy by "putting him down," as though there was no more value left in the little boy—especially the part that responded to his feelings, even when he couldn't identify them. That was my experience growing up, and it may have been similar to yours.

This model of manhood no longer can serve this world. We know now what men long for. We know what they need. No longer can the models of the traditional "machismo" serve us adequately. They aren't enough.

This is the time for you.

## Authenticity and Honesty

For adults, authenticity and honesty are essential to healthy relationships, and to self-respect. Authenticity and honesty begin at a pre-verbal time in the life of the infant, because they experience, in the care they receive, whether the parents chose to bring this child joyfully into the world, or they didn't (or simply couldn't). These choices make a difference in how the child experiences the caretakers.

To create that result in grown men (and women), parents must demonstrate that they have an authentic and honest relationship together, with a willingness to speak the hard truth and the ability to know deep inside themselves what they truly want and need for one another and for their children. Without this honest understanding of their own needs, their needs can't be met. The child's first experiences have everything to do with whether its needs are being met. It can't be explained adequately, but the infant also recognizes when the needs of the parents aren't being met. The infant can feel things without "understanding" them. The infant feels unhappy in the presence of unhappiness, just as surely as it feels soothed in the presence of happiness. Authenticity and honesty are the sources of happiness in relationships.

The relationship needs of infants are met when their survival needs are met. The absence of authenticity and honesty in the relationship of the caretakers creates negative impacts in the life of the child. If the infant's needs aren't met, its first relationship experience is unsuccessful. The modeling that takes place in the early years of life is a building block in the growth process. Children who haven't benefited from effective child rearing practices have no capacity for understanding the basis of adult relationships. The experience of not thriving creates emotional and cognitive deficits. These emotional and cognitive skills are essential for building relationships based in authenticity and honesty.

The child was born to thrive. The child will thrive in the presence of authenticity and honesty. The child will only survive without those things. If you're a father, would you choose for your child to thrive, or just to survive?

## First Steps on the Journey

I recognize that in your healing journey, you don't have to know the details to get to where you need to go. All you need is to want more for yourself. The answers will come as long as you stay open to what is coming from inside you.

I am also aware of my fear that what I say to you here may seem to have no value to you. I am afraid that I will not have an impact on your life. Ultimately I am afraid that I will be alone. As a boy, I only recognized that I was afraid, without understanding and without having learned compassion for myself. Despite all my fears as a grown man, I move towards the light of my being. I take the action that I need to take and recognize the risks of being vulnerable; and still I act. Every journey starts with fear, as well as joy.

Today I'm the mature man I've wanted to be. I share myself as an invitation and as part of my mission on earth, to create a compassionate world by teaching how to live authentically from the heart. For those men who say they have no fears, I say that they perhaps lie to themselves about other things, too. If we disown the very nature of our beings, everything else we see is not as clear, including the lies we tell ourselves.

## The Wonder Years

In my healing journey, I learned that what I thought I wanted to become was a fantasy, an image of someone other than myself. Trying to become someone else did not give me the opportunity to look within myself. I learned that lessons of the heart are always painful. The person I thought I was, was not the authentic me, but someone I made up, from the expectations I took on, as my own, from others. Slowly, gradually, and with openness, I was learning to be my authentic self.

These were hard lessons to learn, understanding that becoming a man was not giving up my inner child but making him part of me, letting him feel alive and valued. I can't make the child disappear. He was meant to be part of me. He is a part of me, even a part of the adult that I am now.

I lived most of my life believing that in order for me to grow, I had to leave my little boy behind. I believed that the grown person would not be the same person as the boy.

Watching the grownups, I taught myself that in order to grow up I needed to give up my feelings. I observed and believed that men never cried. I actually don't remember ever feeling the relief of crying, because of the disapproval others gave me about this. My need to be loved drove all my thoughts and actions as a child, and this need didn't go away as a young man. It isn't just about crying; it's about chipping away at the freedom to be authentic— about doing what I'm feeling. When my actions don't match up with what I'm feeling, I'm not being authentic. Today I'm no longer driven just by powerful outside influences. I can look inside, and I can ask myself, "Is this who I want to be?" I have that choice. I'm my own person, driven from the inside. I'm a man now.

The ways boys are taught to become men differ from one culture to another, but in essence, the results may be the same. It's a process that robs a man of being himself, from being real inside his skin, from knowing and then being able to speak what is true for him. Boys teach themselves to please others, and to conform to the expectations of others; and this early "learning" persists into manhood. The messages that are spoken to the man continue to be both confused and confusing. For example, women frequently want men to be more expressive in relationships; yet the man has taught himself to keep everything inside and not show his emotions. These old lessons fail in adult relationships. This may have pleased the grownups when the man was a boy, but who does it serve for the grown man? It serves nobody.

The early teachings are so powerful that they can only be left behind by a conscious choice. The grown man can choose to make a major change in life, in order to improve his relationships with others and even with himself. To do these things, he must look at the lessons he learned as a child about manhood, and reach a new understanding of the world, based on what the grown man can see and feel. Mind and body work together in this.

## Consequences We Can See

How many sources of unhappiness are connected to the ways we teach boys to be men? We see conflicts between nations, violence in all forms, oppression (both institutionalized and personal), impasses in relationships with intimate partners, distance and unhappiness between a father and his children. Could there be an explanation?

A boy is taught to believe that in order to be a man he must fight and get his way, show his dominance, and not walk away from conflict. He is taught to tough it out, and cut off the human quality that makes him tender, compassionate, fearful, sad, angry, and joyful. He must also cut off his need for others. The child has taught himself that to be a man is to be independent, and to be independent is not to need anything from anyone. He must create and maintain the illusion that he is strong. He must be perceived by others as a man who is not to be "messed with."

For fear that he will be taken advantage of, he must be self-sufficient and rely on his own devices and not ask for help. Asking for help is considered a sign of weakness and not a noble quality for a man to acquire. He must be perfect in maintaining the image of what a man is. He must conquer and win, sometimes at any cost. He must show an image of strength when he feels like falling down on his knees and sobbing like a baby. He must be hard and fearless to project an image of control for himself and others. These are still the fears of the little boy, based on the lessons he taught himself. In essence, men are not allowed to possess any of those qualities that characterized the little boy. Yet these qualities that connect us with our feelings are the qualities that make us human.

Without having the cultural sanctity to show up in authentic ways (in which our actions match our feelings), men can turn inward towards isolation, withdraw from others, or act out in aggression and violence of all forms. A man who disregards his emotions is a ticking bomb; and when he does explode we see destruction and chaos in his family, in his work, and in other personal relationships. Men who are not in touch with their emotional selves are extremely dangerous, since they have no regard for the welfare of others or themselves. If they are not "sensitive," they are not aware of their own feelings, or the feelings of others.

The idea that we are all interdependent and connected at many levels is a foreign concept to these men. If they have no idea of what they can receive from others, they have no idea of how much they can give, simply by acknowledging that we are all connected.

Each of us has a hunger to be loved and cared for. This hunger knows no bounds and has no limitations. It must be met, even as grown adults. It must be met in relationship with other human beings and in relationship to ourselves, because relationships are the key to having a meaningful and fulfilling life. If this need is not met directly, it will usually be met indirectly, showing up as narcissism and self-love and the desire for "power," or some other perverted form of self-gratification.

The human relationship is the fragrance that brings hope to our senses, giving us renewal. It makes our lives more livable, knowing we are ultimately not alone. It can strengthen us to handle our daily struggles, disappointments, and battles of living. It's the current that allows our hearts to be recharged and renewed, day after day, knowing we have a place to return to. It's the music that brings meaning into our lives.

## Authentic Power of Adult Men

I return over and over to the conclusion that healing ourselves as men is not only good for us, but for everyone around us. Men with the power to live as authentic men can improve all of their relationships, because honesty and authenticity are the only sources of hope that conflict can be resolved.

As authentic men, we can live in the world without hiding in our shadows, denying the truth of who we are, without shame for the feelings we have. This is our power, and within it lies the richness of our lives. With this power we can make a real difference in how we live and in the lives we touch. There is only one way to heal ourselves and that is in becoming aware that there is something lacking in us, something missing, something that is not quite right. The paths are many.

Every choice involves risks. We need to know that in revealing our most intimate feelings to others, we risk crossing a line by expecting more intimacy than a person might be comfortable in sharing. Each choice is courageous, because it involves risks. Healing is a choice. It's not magic. It's work. It requires revealing the feelings of the grown man.

This is men's work. Men struggle to accept and then reveal the feelings they experience. Men on a healing path have made the choice to acknowledge that something inside needs attention, needs a closer examination. They are the only ones who can ask the questions that need to be asked. "What am I really feeling, and how can it guide my actions?" Not all men choose to ask the question, because not all men choose to accept the risks. Many of us are afraid to share our feelings, not because we don't want to feel them, but because we have felt rejection before, and we've bought into the lies of the childhood lessons, as a way to feel safe. How many of us know someone who thinks and acts as though there is nothing wrong, when we see a different truth in how they live? How many of us live as though there's nothing wrong, when we can't find a way out of emotional paralysis, our fear of making the next choice?

The question is still, "What am I really feeling, and how can it guide my actions?" Remember, please, that this is the meaning of authenticity—that a person's actions are guided by what they are feeling. Actions and feeling are "in congruity;" when they match, and there is no conflict. This is the meaning of living in authenticity.

Now that that we know the question to be asked, how do we feel (and how do we respond) when some of us say that there is no question to ask and nothing needs fixing, despite the evidence to the contrary?

This is a form of denial. We can't reconcile the incongruity between what we heard as children, and what we've learned as adults. So, we choose to perpetuate the lies that we learned as children, about the kinds of behavior that identify the "legendary man," without regard for the fact that we have learned that these strange requirements are inhuman and dysfunctional. In my judgment, these men remain boys inside, in order to preserve what they've always believed, because it's easier than making their own decisions.

Their effort keeps the lie alive, for them. They continue to disown their power and live out the scripted part of themselves that represents everything they know about how to live as a man. I have seen some of these men die alone, without anyone around them, without anyone visiting them, without anyone touching them. These are types of men that choose not to cry, not to feel. They have no one. Just as their fathers or other adults instructed them, they die as their fathers and grandfathers have often died, perpetuating the cycle of dying alone. A man that chooses to live alone chooses to die alone.

In one form or another, our need for love must be met; we must be loved. It is how we love, how we go about getting the love we need, that determines our healing. The key is that without accepting our need for one another, we ignore our need and act it out in indirect ways. A man who is not loved turns to anger, or isolation, or becomes an addict, or gambles his life savings, or pursues "power," no matter what it looks like, or has countless affairs. The human sense of power can only come from self-fulfillment, from giving and receiving love, love from oneself and love from others. Love is truth. It's in the heart that we humans feel love. It's also the heart that feels empty. Love is energy that fills the heart up. All our efforts toward self-gratification leave us feeling empty.

## What the Future Holds

We are beginning to break the stereotypes of immature masculinity that once were major forces in how we conditioned our boys to become men. Yet, there is much more to go. More can be done as a culture to increase our awareness of developing healthy, honest, authentic, mature masculinity. These are choices, and these choices require courage.

By teaching ourselves within our families the importance of one's personal healing journeys, we are breaking the generational chains that have been passed down from our fathers and grandfathers to us. We can acknowledge that our parents and the generations before them gave us everything that they thought we would need, in order to create full lives for ourselves. With the passing of time, we can be thankful for what they gave, even as we reject parts of their gifts to us.

By becoming aware of who we really are, we can influence in real ways those most significant to us-- the people who we love the most, though we may feel most challenged with them. Our partners, our children, and in our interpersonal relationships, this is where our true selves have the most potential to emerge and bloom. In these relationships, we give meaning to our lives.

When men open up their wounds for the first time, they become authentic human beings, with real emotions, a sense of urgency, and a hunger and need for what they lacked. These are the men that we can all become and relate to in our lives. These are the men who did not cry but yearned to.

The men of tomorrow are the children of today. Today's children are exposed to a very different world than yesterday's children. The challenges of today's children can only be faced with authenticity, with a real openness to what they see, to what they know in their hearts as true. They can only get there, if we honor them fully and show them they can still be men even when they cry.

In this circle of men in which I have always felt I wanted to belong to as a boy, but never belonged to, I now take part as man without leaving my boy behind. Like other men, I was the man who believed I had to be tough. I stuffed all my feelings to prove I was strong. I learned that I can be the man who is loving, honest and vulnerable without feeling threatened in my masculinity.

This is the man I have always thought I could be. This is the man that I am. This is also the man you can be.

# Chapter 4
# The Battle Front: Casualties Worth Saving

## Stories of Hope

For every man who has brought his life to a professional for help, there must be thousands of men who have chosen to continue living the way they've always lived, without finding help, because what they want for themselves seems impossible to reach. Men who come to me in my practice have trusted their lives to me, and I would never violate the sacred trust they have placed in me. For that reason, the names that follow have been changed, and the stories you'll read represent similar events in the lives of many men. The stories of these men were extremely painful. Each of these men has recognized that something was missing in his life, and found the courage to change that fact, one victory at a time.

It doesn't matter where the wound was inflicted, or how profound it was, whether from playing fields to battlefields, or from family or school or religion or peers. Many men carry deep emotional scars. Healing the wounds underneath those scars can still be accomplished by the growing man.

## Paul

His gait was slow and steady. Just like a good soldier who had listened to his Captain, and followed all his orders, he was coming from the front lines like many of his brothers, wounded but alive. Like many men, he did not feel his wounds. I have seen so many like him. He asked where he should sit as though he was waiting for his next order from me.

At 61years old, he sat in my office directly facing me with a stone face. He had just lost his job. Fearing for the loss of his job, and afraid of not being able to find another one, he believed he was too old to be hired. He began talking to me as though I would help him find his next job. He also told me he needed to look for another place to live, because he was having recurring conflicts with his "significant other." Without income, he believed his worst fear might come true—becoming homeless and unloved and alone.

Paul spoke about being afraid and in terror of the unknown, yet he showed no sign of experiencing the fear he was describing. Without my training and intuition to see the obvious, this man gave no signal that he was in a dangerous situation. His stoic presentation did not give the impression of a man whose life was falling apart. He continued talking, sharing how his co-worker was crying when he heard the news that he was also losing his job. Paul approached his co-worker when he saw him crying and said "What good is that going to do?"

Paul understood my invitation and my permission to bring out his feelings and do the same thing his co-worker had done; and he chose to reject the invitation, as he said to me again, "What good is crying going to do?"

I looked at him intently and told him I could not help him find a job, but I could help him get his life back. I knew he had not been successful keeping jobs. He had lost several jobs in the past, not because of layoffs, but because of his angry outbursts with co-workers. That was what prompted him to come to see me.

Paul grew up emotionally beaten down by his father, and no matter how much he tried to please his father; he never measured up. He could not remember his father ever saying anything good about him. Paul thought of his father as an "emotional Nazi," the stereotype of a man who kills with his disapproval.

His father was a very successful businessman, away from home for long periods of time. When he was home, he would constantly put Paul down and criticize him for not measuring up to his expectations. His father had double standards. He demanded that Paul respect him, even though he was inconsiderate of Paul, and insensitive to Paul's emotional needs. Paul's mother had only one way to protect Paul from his father's severe emotional abuse, and that was to tell Paul to listen to what his father said, not what he did. Of course, these contradictory messages confused Paul even more.

Paul did not have any sense of safety and refuge as a child. His survival instinct was to obey and do what his father told him. There were no questions asked, and he tried very hard to be a good boy, without understanding what that meant.

The man who sat in my office was not a man inside. He was still just a little boy who never grew up to be the man he could be. When things went badly in his adult life, he acted like his father towards others, threatening his co-workers to create fear and confusion, where he wanted respect. Most times when he became angry and demanding it was disproportionate to any response that could improve the situation, in the work setting and in his personal life. Constantly feeling threatened in his fragile sense of personal power, his only way of achieving consensus was to make demands. Co-workers heard his demands and resented them, and passively sabotaged Paul's efforts to make the plans succeed. When Paul expressed his anger it created more problems for him, and resulted in mismanagement of his subordinates. His anger became unmanageable when he grabbed a worker by his collar. His conduct was written up, and he was told to seek therapy.

This was a man that learned at a very early age to "bottle up" all of his feelings except anger. Anger was the only feeling that he knew how to express and felt safe with. Yet, it got him into trouble. Expressing anger gave him a feeling of personal power. He felt that this was the only way he could be heard.

Paul also described that he felt "he was always wrong." It seemed as though he couldn't possibly be doing "the right thing," except when he was angry. Only when he was angry did he sense that his actions matched up with what he was actually feeling.

Paul was never taught to have the full spectrum of emotions that men need to express fully, in mature masculinity. Since his feelings had been repressed and denied, he lacked confidence and had very little self worth. It was only when he was ranting and raving that he experienced a feeling of power that he could exercise. He rationalized his treatment of others by blaming them for his own conduct. If only they would listen to his instructions, he would not get so angry.

This became clear to me: Until Paul allowed himself to feel the effects of having had a father whose actions created an unspoken rule that anger is the only acceptable feeling, Paul could not experience a feeling of his personal power in any other way; and nothing in his life would change. His healing work was to transform his inner self from being a victim to owning the pain of not being seen or heard by his father, and most of all to accept every aspect of him.

Owning and accepting what he denied and repressed was the key to becoming whole. The man needs to reconnect with the pain he didn't permit himself to feel as a child. By going back to his actual experience, he can get the feedback from his body that permits him to trust his own experience and to trust himself. Paul's reclaiming of his wound by his father would validate his experience and give him the power of feeling and being fully human.

There is no more powerful human force than taking back your self. Paul needed to own his rage and his feelings of abandonment by his father, his need for the blessings of his father that were never received, and finally to grieve the father he never had and still hungered for. As he grieved this relationship, he would begin to forgive his father and himself. Part of this forgiveness would require acknowledging the positive qualities that his father had shown, and those that are similar to his own positive qualities.

As he sat facing me, I looked at him as though it was his last day to live as a "victim" and start to choose living in as a man who accepts himself. This was his moment of truth, the challenge to face himself as he really was and not what he thought he ought to be. He was ready to "die" symbolically by doing what he had been avoiding for more than 50 years of his life.

My intention was to support him by seeing him as he truly was. This complete form of attention seemed both unexpected and uncomfortable for Paul, possibly because he might never have experienced it before. His most frequent experience was still discomfort, the same feeling he got whenever he had no response for something that was happening to him—the feeling that he was always somehow "wrong." He was used to feeling uncomfortable within his own skin. He didn't know any other way to feel.

Using a direct and caring approach, my words pierced Paul's defenses as I said, "Boys don't cry, but men do". He instantly looked puzzled. Then his stare deepened as his shoulders dropped and he took another deep breath. He truly had no response for what he was experiencing at that moment, and he knew it. I then said, "You need to see yourself now as someone who is having a heart attack or another life-ending experience. You have a choice to make. You can continue on the same path you've been on, and eventually die unfulfilled and broken-hearted and follow your father's footsteps. Or you can choose another path as the man you were meant to be. Your job is to take back what you've given up."

I put this choice to men frequently to reveal a "lie" that they're living; and the lie is that they can only live the same way they've always lived. "Are you willing to do whatever it takes to heal and become a man?" No man that I have worked with has ever said "no" to that question. That would be an "un-manly" thing to say. The boy feels the challenge, but it's the man that actually gets it done. It takes discipline, commitment, and intention. This can only come from masculine maturity. Together, we use their old mythology to the advantage of the man who is struggling.

"What do I need to do?" Or "It depends on what I need to do." Either of those answers is enough for us to move into an agreement. What they don't know at that time is they don't need to do a thing. They just need to let go of everything that they believed was true, so that they can learn it in a new way. They do have to hang on tight, for this hard part of their journey.

Paul had been living out the messages and myths he was taught by his father, and he was taking them to his grave. One was the belief that a man doesn't cry. He was told that a man sucks up his feelings and moves on without letting a feeling actually happen. I explained to Paul that this is exactly what boys do, and it isn't what grown men do. "Are you willing to do what real men do?"

Again I challenged his mythology. This is not for boys. Boys don't do this kind of work. "Are you willing to do whatever it takes to do it?" He was ready. He said "yes." At a time like this, I recognize that a man needs to get in touch with his feelings, in order to expose them and experience them.

I got two oversized pillows and told him to kneel on the floor. I instructed him to bring his fists together and begin breathing diaphragmatically. Then, making a fist and with intention, I invited him to begin hitting the pillows like he was taking something back from a bully. As he followed my directions, I sensed he needed to stop suffering in silence. I asked him to say "You're killing me, you're killing me," out loud. He began shouting these words several times without any hesitation. Since these were my words and not his, I asked him whether these words fit for him. In a strong decisive voice he said "no." "So what does fit?"

"You don't understand," he said. I asked him to say that instead, and he did.

Paul's body and facial expression began shifting. He was becoming more alive in front of me. Instantly he was being the boy he never allowed himself to be, expressing words he never allowed himself to say. He was terrified to say those words when he was a child. He was safe to speak them now, after 50 years. He began crying the tears that kept him locked up. Now for the first time he felt the words his dad said to him. For the first time, he entered the place where men can access their true feelings and many boys feel the need to hide. He began grieving his life, for all that came to pass, for all that was taken away from him, and for all that he was finally getting back. The sense of relief was evident in his face. He had done something he had never done before—he let his feelings match his actions. His feeling and actions were "in congruity." He was behaving "authentically" for the first time. His growth as a mature man began.

## Robert

When I first saw Robert, he seemed almost invisible. As he shook my hand, it felt as though I was shaking someone's hand for the last time. He was depressed, and his eyes barely made contact with mine. As he spoke he smirked, undercutting the significance and the meaning of his words. His way of speaking drew my attention because men who come to see me in my practice almost never feel light-hearted. That isn't how they feel when they need help and are struggling to ask for it. Robert spoke to me as though his words might receive a hurtful response if he failed to use this form of protective "armor" in conversation. The mismatch of his sweaty palm and his facial gestures was a clear contradiction, and he was obviously unconscious of the "lie" he was communicating in this mismatch of behavior and words.

At 38 years of age, married for seven years, with two young children and a job in sales that felt very stressful to him, Robert spoke apologetically, as though he had done something wrong. He revealed that he was having an affair with a woman he met on the road in his work travels, and his marriage was falling apart. He had difficulty opening up to his wife. Robert felt that his wife was very demanding of his time, and he felt totally misunderstood. Their sexual relationship deteriorated from the family stresses of taking care of children, working, and just feeling tired. He did not have energy for himself and felt compromised, feeling guilty and judging that he was not doing enough for his family. His wife also was very busy working, with not enough time to be together, and both were trying to make ends meet. Late nights for him were typical, with meetings and business drinking in a pattern of heavy alcohol consumption.

He had a family history of alcoholism. His father died from it when he was 64. When Robert spoke of his father, pain was evident in his eyes. His look of bewilderment and shallow breathing signaled his emotional distress. When Robert was a child, his father wasn't "there" for him. Robert wasn't ready to hear this truth, since our relationship was still not "safe" enough to contain this emotional truth about his father. Perhaps he knew it but wouldn't say it. He seemed very confused about his actions. He said he loved his wife and his children, but something was missing in his life. His affair made him feel wanted and cared for, but he knew it was not the right thing to do. He felt guilty and ashamed for what he was doing. His wife did not even know he came to see me.

Robert went to see his doctor before seeing me, because he had difficulty sleeping. His doctor prescribed medication and told him to see me. He had never been in psychotherapy and had many misconceptions about it. He had always taken care of his own affairs till now. That was what he was taught to do.

Further conversation revealed that Robert's parents were divorced when he was in his teens. There were gaps in his family history, even though I knew he was convinced he was telling me his entire truth. He had a strong suspicion that both of his parents were unfaithful to each other. His mother was still living, but their relationship was not close. He had an older sister, with whom he spoke sporadically. There was one thread that kept surfacing throughout his sharing of his history. He felt unwanted somehow, even though he said his parents loved him. These two statements, together, were an important contradiction that couldn't be ignored. I felt certain that if Robert was going to "rebuild his life" in a new way, he had to go back to what he was running from for most of his life. At this point, I sensed that the contradiction he had spoken could only be resolved by reconnecting with his earliest feelings of being disconnected-- in his family of origin.

"Who loves you?" When I asked that question, I was not asking it in order for him to give me an answer. I asked him this question as a means of provoking his defenses. This particular question was a basic but fundamental piece of the healing, as a direct route to his feelings of disconnection. The question provided a way to open the door to his emotional work. In order for him to do this work, it was necessary to bring out his inner child-- the little boy that felt unloved. This grown man was afraid to know it; and this produced a lot of shame, as it always does.

All boys want to be loved, and they need to be loved. In Robert's history, he witnessed and experienced a slew of unloving situations. His father and mother were unavailable to provide for his emotional needs; they couldn't even meet one another's emotional needs. Their marriage was a burden for him. As a child, he had to repress or withhold or deny his needs. There was not enough "caring" to go around. He perceived both of his parents to be very needy, and he felt he needed to take care of them, as children do. By taking care of them, he thought unconsciously that they would take care of him. Of course, that never happened; and it rarely does in situations like his.

This form of taking care of the adults is an unconscious survival mechanism. In response to their early perception of this "danger," children draw on their own early experiences of having been soothed. When the parents have no capacity for understanding the inner experiences of their children, then the children invent an explanation. The explanation is usually egocentric and false-- that the child is somehow responsible for the conflict. When the child attempts a rescue from the danger he perceives, the parents are unable to recognize or understand the initiative from their children. Often these efforts are turned away in ways that are emotionally abusive, and sometimes emotionally brutal. Whatever form it takes, the child experiences being turned away as disconnection.

Robert's healing would require that he become conscious in some way that he was powerless as a child.

Although children can't understand every detail of complex family dynamics, they often have the ability at an early age to recognize when grown-ups are experiencing emotional pain, even though they don't have the cognitive comprehension of the conflict between their parents. They feel it in their bodies. From that moment of understanding, Robert could choose to stop being powerless in his life by making the decision to stop living as though he's still the powerless child. Robert's experience as a child was like drowning in the chaotic life his parents created for him. Robert's parents gave him no comfort in this dilemma. By the very nature of the dependency needs he had for his parents, he was unable to separate himself from his family chaos. The only way to survive was to deny (unconsciously) the pain he felt, to avoid his own fear of being left alone and abandoned. The grown man can choose to recognize that pain, and learn that even with his fear of abandonment, he can still get his needs met. The familiar fear doesn't have to result in the same isolating response that was familiar to the child. He can find a new way of understanding this part of his life, and the actions he can take to connect with the ones he cares about.

When Robert heard his parents yelling at each other, he would go into his room, shut the door and stay there for hours. No one would see what he was doing, or ask him anything related to why he went to his room. Sometimes he thought they were fighting because of him. This is where Robert began cutting off from his feelings and began to use elaborate fantasies to escape his reality. In times of fear, the "senses" that allow us to regulate how we view the world become flawed. It's like traveling on a road and suddenly being unable to see where you're going, because all of the sudden the rain pours down and it's impossible to see clearly.

Robert's parents were too focused on their own neglected needs to take care of him. His parents never asked the question I was asking, or, for that matter, understood or cared about what he might be feeling when they fought. Parents who do not validate the inner experiences of their children create children who will learn by example to disempower or "turn off" their feelings. This is how boys learn to remain boys. Without feeling acknowledged, the boy remains disempowered and continues to withhold full recognition of what he is feeling. Consequently, boys remain boys emotionally, even as they grow.

Robert looked perplexed when I asked "Who loved you?" He frowned as though he was in serious thought. For a moment I thought he would not answer my question and again his phony smile came on. "My parents gave me everything I wanted," he said. "That wasn't my question. Who loves you?" I asked again. His appearance became more serious as he asked, "Are you saying my parents didn't love me? Or they didn't love me the way I wanted them to love me?"

I asked how Robert was feeling at that moment, because I knew that my question was for his little boy to answer; and I knew his little boy was wounded.

"I feel confused." This was a typical answer I get from many men who don't really know how they feel. He began touching the corner of one of his eyes, which told me his body was achieving congruency with what he was feeling. "Your eyes are getting watery. What do you think your eyes are trying to tell you?" "I feel like crying but I'm holding myself back," Robert said.

After a moment I spoke the words that I speak often with men doing their personal work. "Robert, this is men's work. Cry if that's what you're feeling. Boys don't feel they have permission to cry; but men don't have to ask for approval or permission. They can cry, and sometimes they do."

The dam opened. Robert placed both hands over his face, as though he wanted to hide from me, from the sad truth he began feeling; and he started crying. I let him know, by my silence, that he was in a safe place for doing this work. When Robert had cried without stopping for several minutes, he had touched a source of disconnection and pain for the first time. For the first time, he had the experience of validating his own feelings instead of denying them. He had started the work of becoming a man who can recognize his feelings, and act on them without fear of disapproval.

# Tony

When I met Tony for the first time in my office, I noticed immediately that he was trying to get me to laugh at his initial remarks. This is how Tony approached most things he was anxious about. He made up jokes.

Each of us has our own style of approaching something new. For him to feel safe, he needed to know that I found him funny. Perhaps then, I would not emotionally reject him. Fear of rejection is one of the deepest fears that humans carry. Tony was a great storyteller; he always had something funny to say.

Tony was in his second marriage, and in his early 50's. He was a highly intelligent and articulate individual. He had a Ph.D. degree in chemistry and had taught for many years at the university level. When I met him, he reported that he was working as a freelance photographer. He was a recovering alcoholic, but didn't attend A.A. meetings. His first marriage had failed due to drinking. When he finally stopped drinking and began to pay attention to his relationships, his wife was emotionally out of the marriage. He had two grown children from his first marriage.

Tony wasn't one of the men who have a problem talking about themselves, feeling uneasy as they sit for the first time in a therapist's office, not sure what to say. Tony had lots to say. I needed to let Tony talk, but I was also conscious of the limited amount of time we had in our first session and needed to get down to business. Behind the stories about his job, his previous marriage, and even earlier times he went to treatment with his first wife to try to save his marriage, I wasn't understanding the "burn" he was feeling right now—the reason why he was in my office at this particular time. When I finally interrupted, he quickly became more subdued. His body seemed to sit further back and his eyes widened. He said he was feeling depressed, going through life without feeling much enjoyment. He did have a passion for taking pictures but found dealing with people to be a hassle. He was a bit overweight; but overall he felt healthy, even though he didn't take good care of himself physically. His philosophy was why fix it if it wasn't broken. He didn't believe in preventive care.

The truth was that he didn't care much for himself. He would go out of this way to help someone else, though. This was a man who seemed to be very friendly, and who would not have problems getting along with others. He was a likeable individual who made others feel at ease and safe; and spending time with Tony probably felt good for everybody who knew him. I kept asking myself, "Why is he here?" I asked him for more information about his family, and began to see the reason.

Tony's father was a lawyer, and he was good at what he did. He had flair about him, too, and juries liked him. He was dramatic and had an eloquent way of speaking. He was also an alcoholic who consumed sufficiently large amounts of alcohol daily that he was intoxicated when he woke up in the morning. Though he was also diabetic, Tony reported that it never interfered with his father's overeating and his love for his booze. He loved his wife but was never around to show it. Tony also remembered that his father was never around for him, and he remembered making excuses to his friends when his father arrived drunk to pick him up from school.

Tony's face dropped as he recalled how his mother tried to get his father to quit drinking, and this was something he vividly remembered. When Tony was six, his mother fell down the stairs of their home and broke her leg. Tony blamed himself for the accident because she slipped on a Catechism book that he left on the stairs. A year after this accident, his mother started complaining about pains in her legs and back and began receiving radiation treatment. Though he couldn't really understand the meaning of what was going on, he did find out that she had cervical cancer.

Tony continued to share his history without any emotion. He could have been telling me a story about someone else's life, for that matter, since it was not apparent from his presentation that it really mattered to him. He was about eight years old when his mother began to get a combination of radiation and surgery and was spending more and more time at home, in a great deal of pain. He was, as he said, "instructed to give his mother morphine injections and was cautioned never to exceed the upper limit, even if she begged him." Just listening to his story, I was shocked at the inappropriateness of that responsibility on the shoulders of a child. And when he was 12 years old, she began begging him to give him more morphine; and he refused.

Tony was getting unspoken "messages" that his mother was relying on him to "be the man of the family," and then she became very disappointed in him for not stepping up to help his mother from her pain. He continued to recall that he was torn between his obligation to his mother and the fear of burning in eternal hell if he did what he considered "the right thing," which I equated with "ending her suffering." His mother died a year later, a week before Christmas, when she was only 53 years old. Tony shared that he and his uncle together arranged her wake, her funeral and headstone. Through all this, he had tried to show no emotion, and tried to comfort his father, who (to his surprise) was more sober than usual, though he was "an emotional mess."

This piece of Tony's life was frozen in time, deep in his being. This unmoved boy had appeared to become a hero on the outside; but on the inside he stayed frozen in time. He was trapped between feeling unloved by his mother and going to hell if he caused her death by ending her suffering. How was this man holding the conflict of this reality in his psyche? And how can a little boy go on with his life this way?

Tony, in session, was unaware that when his mother died, a piece of him had died too as he buried her. He didn't hear the words that a 12-year old boy would need to hear at such a time. "You didn't kill your mother. She was very ill, and her body couldn't be kept alive any longer. What you did for your mother was an act of love. You did your best. You are an incredibly courageous little boy. It's okay to cry, Tony. You loved your mother very much, and by taking care of her you actually did keep her alive as long as anyone could."

These words or words like these were not said to Tony. Instead Tony took care of himself by doing what most children do when they have inadequate parental instruction and support during critical times. Tony took on all the responsibility for his mother's life and death, and decided that his mother's death was his fault. Tony throughout his life did not take good care of himself, and this inaction was a passive way of killing himself. The grown man wasn't alive in him, and Tony was still a little boy frozen in time underneath his "accomplishments." He simply knew he didn't feel alive, and didn't know why.

Being with Tony was a disarming experience. He made himself liked. Since he was a bit overweight, I asked him when he saw a doctor the last time. He did not remember, and asked "Why fix something if it's not broken?" Tony's façade was evident to a trained eye. Tony had previous therapy, and he said not much had been accomplished. They did a lot of talking, which for Tony was an effective "defensive" response. Tony had learned very early that talking his way out of things would help him survive. If I was going to help Tony to choose living instead of dying, I needed to help him find the myth that was embedded in his being, and drove most of his actions towards inertia. The myth was that he could have kept his mother alive.

During the course of treatment with Tony, he began telling the truth-- the truth of his real life. It was not so much what he said that mattered, but how he said it. It was also necessary to decode and interpret his body language, to help him be congruent. He began to reveal that he couldn't be fully alive, because his mother wasn't alive. Another necessary piece was to help him recognize that what he experienced as a truth response in his body was something different from an intellectual insightful connection. Tony was very bright, but his intelligence wouldn't help him here. He had to remember how to see the world the way the 12-year old child saw it. Only in that would he find freedom.

It took almost a year for Tony to begin to recognize that he was worthy of love just for who he was and not for what he did. Throughout my course of treatment with Tony, I was supportive and loving but firm. I challenged him when his actions didn't appear to match his feelings; and it was always a "red flag" for me when his humor came up as armor. He began to feel safer and safer with me because he knew I expected him to be authentic. I wouldn't permit him to continue protecting himself with humor, so that he could avoid feeling his emotions. Once he realized that I would not settle for anything other than his real self, he began to show himself. He became more curious and began to rely less on humor as his sidekick.

Tony's reluctance to see a medical doctor alarmed me from the start because it looked like an adult form of the self-sacrifice he had taken on as a child. When he went to see a doctor for the first time in years, the doctor confirmed that Tony had a long history of dysthymia, a lack of ability to enjoy. He was not clinically depressed but had a chronic depressive mood.

When Tony was placed on medications, he began to feel better. He began to pursue other interests and became curious about other forms of personal growth work. He joined a men's group and began to participate and involve himself with other men who were also on the path of healing. At this later phase of his treatment he brought in his wife, so that they could work on their marriage.

By this time, Tony had begun living life in the present. He felt alive. He had hopes for the future. Tony had learned to see the difference between self-denial and self-sacrifice—to see that self-denial is temporary, and self-sacrifice is as permanent as death, until a man chooses to live. He also learned how to see the experiences of his childhood through the eyes of a grown man, so that he could treat himself as being worthy of the same amount of love and care that he had been able to provide to his mother.

## Carlos

He shook my hand and smiled. His hands were clammy and sweaty. I sensed his embarrassment and discomfort, and knew immediately that I was meeting the child in Carlos, as well as the man. He sat down and looked at me with his Hispanic black eyes, waiting for me to start the conversation. He was 42 years old, single, separated from his wife for three years. He had one daughter who was living with her mother.

He said he was referred by a female therapist because he was uncomfortable sharing his story with a woman therapist. He was molested when he was six years old, by his father's friend. His parents divorced when he was young, and he lived with his father in Mexico. Because of his previous therapeutic experience he knew what to expect from the initial visit. Yet he did not know what he had to do, in order to heal.

Carlos always felt he didn't measure up as a man. He was not sure if he was gay, bisexual or heterosexual. He reported that he had never had a homosexual experience, but felt drawn to men as much as he did to women. He said that one of the reasons why his parents divorced was that his father was gay. His father brought men to his house when he was growing up. Carlos was an attractive Hispanic male who did not seem to have difficulties finding women. The problem was that he did not know his sexual identity and had a severe level of anxiety. He had a very soft side to himself that was uncommon for the macho-driven Hispanic culture he grew up in. He was also highly confused and depressed. Carlos was ambitious and self-driven, and he wanted to open up a restaurant. Lacking a real sense of himself, he felt greatly tormented.

Carlos had an immediate connection with me. It seemed he needed a firm and caring male who would create a safe place for him to explore the demons of his past. As the therapy progressed, Carlos became more comfortable with me and began to reveal where he felt stuck the most. He became emotionally numb when he was sexually molested at 10 years old. He recalled that he was walking on a farm road where his father lived and saw one of his old cousins walking towards him with another friend of his. His cousin was in his late teens or early twenties. They knew each other as an extended family but they were not close. His cousin and his friend approached him and began talking to him. They walked off a path, where his cousin and his friend told him to take off his pants and they were going to sodomize him. He told him he did not want to; and the next thing he knew they grabbed him and took his pants down and each took turns sodomizing him. They said that if he told anyone, they would hurt his mother and him. Feeling ashamed, he walked home alone. His mother noticed some blood stains in his pants, and he said he fell down on the road. He never told anyone the truth about this.

Carlos needed to begin taking back the power he lost when the rape occurred. In that moment, he was trapped and physically incapable of defending himself. In therapy, he participated in a group psychodrama and was able to replay the rape in detail. This time he symbolically killed his perpetrator and took back the power he was repressing. His self-hatred, coupled with deep feelings of shame and guilt, had prevented Carlos from moving forward. By feeling his rage towards the perpetrators and acting it out in a safe place, he was able to regain his power, in a sense of being in control of outcomes.

Power comes from within. Carlos felt helpless because his feelings were locked up inside. As he developed trust in our relationship, he felt safe to be the boy he was not able to be, after he was raped. He took back his power. Carlos eventually was able to know who he was, as a grown man; and he developed a loving relationship that grew into marriage.

## Growing into Healthy Masculine Maturity

The men you've just met shared many similarities in their boyhoods and in their work to grow into men with a healthy and mature sense of who they are as men. Understand that their stories represent extreme situations. Understand, too, that many men fail to learn these same lessons in their boyhoods, for reasons that are far less traumatic. Every man who feels that something important is missing in his life can benefit from hearing the successes of the men who have shared their stories.

Among these men, each recognized that something was missing in his life. Each realized that all of his previous efforts had failed to find what was missing, and made the decision to look for help. As a result of developing trust in someone else, each was able to identify emotions that he had habitually blocked. As each man permitted himself to feel the emotions that had been denied for so long, he was able to "unlearn" some of the old information he had always believed, so that he could approach his life in new ways.

Each also learned that every man is responsible for his own happiness in life, and can create it by asking for what he needs. These are the lessons that men learn as they enter mature masculinity. Every man can choose to continue his growth.

# Chapter 5
# The Making of a Man:  The Lies...

## The Lies Begin Here.

In too many cases, our culture does an awful job in preparing boys to become men.  Many of the problems affecting men today are the results of their early upbringing.  As adults, too many men are ill equipped to have mature relationships with their significant others, to become responsible fathers, and to live in authenticity.

As parents, we start lying to our children in infancy, because we want to protect them from the cruelty of the world.  We create the benevolent archetypes of Santa Claus and the Easter Bunny and the Tooth Fairy because we want our children to have a belief that the world is a kind and gentle place.  We bring these characters into the lives of children from motivations that are positive and loving. We even bring the older children into these lies, with promises to "keep the secret."  We protect our children in these ways because we love them, and we want them to have hope, knowing that hope can be hard to maintain.  We pass on these "lies" because we want our children to enjoy the moments that we experienced as children, and that we remember most fondly.

The message that we create is that some lies are okay.  Each of us makes the choice with our children about which lies are okay to tell, for the protection of our children.  We create for them a magical world of Santa and the Tooth Fairy in order to bring joy and hope and magical possibilities into the lives of children.  We choose the time carefully for explaining about poverty and racism and war, in order to protect them at a time when we feel they need protection. Most would agree that it's a parent's responsibility to protect their children, even from the reality of the world, until the child's understanding of the world is sufficient, cognitively and emotionally, that the children have begun to ask the questions that will permit them to learn about these things, without being frightened or harmed.

As parents, we also tell our children about things that were true in our lives that we want not to be true in their lives.

We tell them it's a cruel hard world, because we've experienced cruelty in our lives. We tell them that they can't trust anybody, because we've been disappointed so many times. We tell them that "boys don't cry," because we believe that it's dangerous to show emotion. We also tell them these things to protect them, so that their lives will be better than the lives that we've had. The message may result from loving protection; but it may also be a reflection of the way we've viewed the world, and it may not be true for them. It may be a lie, and they might believe it, instead of going out into the world to create their own happiness. These are among the lies that harm children.

Early in their upbringing, boys begin to equate the feeling of being "grown up" with the moments when they believe that they have shown themselves to be "better" than others. This shows up in their play, and later in their sexual conquests, and in achieving economic success. Of course, none of these activities makes a man any more mature. The more he compares himself with others, the greater his need for favorable comparison will become. His desires to be better are never satisfied, and there is no true, lasting satisfaction in feeding the ego in these ways.

The false belief in successful competition as a step toward maturity actually leads boys into living life in isolation and seclusion. Their conquests bring only short-lived satisfaction, because all these activities feed the immature ego, and none of them feeds the soul.

The grown man lives in the soul, rather than in the ego. The soul is larger. It includes consciousness that we are all connected. It includes consciousness that we are capable of gifts that will outlive our days. It includes awareness that our actions will have consequences greater than we can easily imagine.

## Living in Ego

Our culture has witnessed extremes of corporate corruption. Top corporate executives have made themselves enormously rich through activities that haven't always met the standards of honesty or lawfulness or fair play, among others. They sometimes demonstrate an attitude that these principles do not apply to them. Rather than being stewards of wealth for the welfare of others, they may have fed themselves and lined their pockets. When these executives have finally been brought to account for their illegal actions, they have blamed others for their corruption. They've shown no mature comprehension of personal responsibility in illegal conduct, and no comprehension of the effects that their self-serving behavior has had on others.

A mature man cares about the lives of others. He doesn't just care about himself.

We must tear down the lies about what defines a mature man. A mature man has the capacity to value his life in terms of his relationships with others. He has the capacity to engage in partnerships with others, partnership with his spouse, with his children, with his co-workers and friends. He shares and takes an active role in the lives of others. The question these men ask themselves is not how much they have in terms of wealth or possessions. Instead they ask "What is my capacity for love in my life with the people I care most about? What type of a partner am I? What type of a father am I? What kind of friend am I? What can I give of myself?" These are the real issues in the lives of mature men, living in ways that model mature masculinity.

When a man examines his life in his later years, what becomes most important is the "mark" he leaves, the difference he made in the lives of others. In the final analysis, a mature man measures his life by how deeply he has loved others.

## Separating Truth and Lies

Like the men you met in the previous chapter, most men are indoctrinated to repress and deny their authentic selves. The boy's earliest passage into manhood begins when others begin imposing their power and will upon the boy, in the form of stated expectations, and in approval given and approval withheld.

These early, yet very powerful, influences imprint all the necessary "soft wiring," propelling boys to fulfill all the expectations of the earliest messages they "perceived" as children. The boy unconsciously integrates the expectations of the adults in his life. He anticipates their approval and disapproval, and acts accordingly. He does not feel this as being oppressed by his caretakers and other adults in his life. He wants to be loved; and his earliest recognition of how to get this love is by conforming to the demands and wants of the adults in his life.

The adults may or may not intentionally know what they are doing to the child. Though most parents are doing the best they can, many lack an understanding of child development, and many repeat the mistakes made by their own parents. The boy's need is to get the love of his caretakers, and he will do whatever it takes to get it. He quickly learns to react and adjust accordingly to the expectations of his caretakers. His need to get the love is paramount to everything he does as a child. Unless the parents of young boys are aware of this powerful drive to feel loved, the conscious (and sometimes unconscious) actions of the parents will take on some of the qualities that oppressed them in their own childhoods. Without the feeling of having received the love they wanted, adults grow physically beyond childhood with the feeling that something is missing. They may become oppressive in their relationships with women, men, and children (and in their roles as partners and parents) as they continue their struggle to feel what they've been missing. Their behavior repeats the harm that was done to them.

The infant has an unstoppable urge to learn, and an overwhelming urge to experience closeness with his (or her) caregivers. The child beyond infancy knows that "something is missing" when demands are made that can't be met, and when approval is withheld without apparent cause. This continued feeling that something is missing is assimilated into the life of a boy who is asked continually to be something that he doesn't know how to be.

This assimilation takes place whether the boy comes from wealth or poverty. The boy (and then the man) looks at the world and doesn't understand what makes up a man, no matter how many times he hears the messages, because he has tried to make his behavior match the messages, and he still knows that something is missing. The messages are the same: "Men are tough. Self-sacrifice is heroic. Men don't show emotions in front of others. Toughen up. If you want something done, do it yourself. You must be able to do it alone. Don't depend on anyone for anything. Winning is everything. Second best is the same as finishing last."

It's time to sort out the lies and the truths about growing into manhood and being a man. This is where the work begins.

## Boys in our Culture

Our culture reinforces oppressive and male-chauvinistic values that are among the "old" ways of making boys into men. In the field of technology one way that these values are sold for consumption by boys is through software games. Many of the computer games in the market teach children to be competitive, where the goal is to win at any cost. The good guys versus the bad guys, the rough and tough characters we see on computer games, and all forms of printed media and television, burn the psyche with the message that no matter what, a man must stay in control. He's on top, but only when he's winning. Many of the software games are models of emotional brutality, filled with monsters and enemies and an ethic that says "kill or be killed." What lessons do these games teach?

As boys grow, play becomes competition. As competition becomes less like play and more like a fight, many boys learn to respond even more aggressively when they realize aggression is being directed at them. Boys face the same choice over and over as they grow: Do I increase the level of aggression and risk a fight, or do I choose to run away?

In response to that question, many boys who lack skill at soothing themselves will often withdraw into a world of isolation. A boy has no outlet because he has no capacity to process emotions. Isolation is a mechanism for "self-soothing." Without self-soothing, a man (or boy) can't regulate or reduce his stress level enough to find a way to see this experience and compare it to other similar experiences. By isolating, a person attempts to soothe himself by putting a stop to the painful experience that he feels in connection with others.

Like isolation, aggression is also an attempt at self-soothing; and it takes the form of attempting to gain less painful feedback from others, even if it's necessary to provoke the reaction. Too frequently, these provocative responses become the relationship with the rest of the world. Isolation is being alone, and a provocative reaction against being alone is quickly identified as aggressive behavior. This is how men keep others at a distance, possibly through the use of sarcasm or (possibly) disrespectful humor. The behavior of a provocative man usually repels the people he interacts with. Aggression toward others will never bring people into closer relationships.

The bombardment of predominantly negative messages by the culture further cuts off the human quality of boys. It doesn't stress cooperative skills, social skills, self-care, and caring for others. The interpersonal processes are rarely taught. An additional "value" is also not taught often enough-- that we need one another not only to survive as a species, but to thrive as a culture. How many men have received guidance about being in relationships or partnerships with others? In the current culture, the focus is not so much about developing strong and lasting relationships. It's more about what a man (or woman) can get from a relationship. Looking for love can become less important than finding a sexual partner. And a man who hasn't experienced strong relationships may continue to increase the number of "intimate" partners he has had, without learning that emotional intimacy is something that only happens within strong relationships.

Without an awareness of interdependence, the boy's frame of reference is that others are there to serve him. Others are not part of his world. They are part of his world only where he can use others to achieve what he wants. He is a taker. It's no coincidence that most of the violence in our society is perpetrated by men. Until men in leadership positions will teach mature masculinity, the cycle will continue to create men with no real sense of authentic power.

Authentic power is the willingness to understand that a man's capacity for feelings, and the willingness to act in response to those feelings, is all that a man can do—and it's enough. The immature understanding of the world continues to think that personal power is gained by taking power from others.

## Unsafe Men

When a man is disconnected, he is cut off from his feelings and unable to understand feedback from himself. He can only recognize his own needs if he can identify his own feelings. Without this feedback, a man is utterly lost in his world. He does not operate from his emotional self, but by outside influences that he has no control over. He doesn't know the meaning of personal power—that he can only control his own responses. His preoccupation is the world of things, not beings, and usually not relationships. Furthermore, he may not have any clue about what drives him. These ghosts are ancient; and man's tendency to deny and repress what is real inside him was part of what he was told to become. His idea of what a man is came from his earliest impressions that have been burned into his mind since he was a very small child. Provocative aggression is the essence of the dangerous man.

A man who does not know what he feels is not a safe man; and therefore he cannot protect himself or others. He does not know how to create safety for himself. He does not know the meaning of the word "safety," and he has no association to this experience. He may believe that it's not supposed to feel safe to be a man. He has to be a man that can deal with danger. Danger and being a man fit like a hand in a glove. Culture creates models of men who combine human attributes with "superhuman" traits like super-strength or the ability to fly, resulting in characters that look as familiar as Superman. The special effects on movie screens rarely show such a superman dying; and boys identify with that. Boys (and immature men) fail to connect with attributes like compassion and mercy and "higher purpose" and respect for all people. They see part of what is on the screen. They see only that a superman is a man's man.

He's invincible. He doesn't know fear. He creates peak experiences to prove his virility. Without masculine maturity, a man can only see part of the picture of manhood.

A man who does not have the capacity to know when he is afraid will choose actions that are an unconscious reaction to his fear. Unconscious fear reactions are rarely constructive. A man unable to identify his fear may act with aggression towards others to protect himself from dangers he can barely identify. He is overloaded with unconscious fear. He becomes hypersensitive to any perceived threat. A question someone may ask can be perceived as a challenge. A comment can be interpreted as a confrontation, in this fragile sense of self. Such a man was taught only to protect himself, and that is what he will do. When a man protects his fear, it is rarely useful to the man or to others. His fear will create further bridges, and isolate him from the ones he needs the most. He will hide and withdraw from contact. The higher the threat the deeper the isolation he will create, separating himself from others. In the extreme range of isolation, men lose touch with those whom they love most, and respond with violent and aggressive acts when they fear loss of control.

Our culture distorts manhood when it invents "powers" that originate in imagination, rather than reality. Some of us are familiar with the term the "flying boy," the boy who imagines that he can fly. We know that anything that flies sooner or later needs to come down, even creatures with wings. The man who was the current Superman character in our time recently died, after years as a paraplegic. He did what most men would barely dare imagine. After the riding accident that seemingly ended his mobility, Christopher Reeve became more of a model of the mature man's capacity for attaining what seems impossible than almost any other man. His life will continue to inspire others to live each day fully. He modeled for the world that being human is really about staying connected with the best qualities that humans can possess, including love and compassion. In that way, he truly was a "super man."

## Body Talk

Our bodies are constantly giving us signals about what we are feeling emotionally. Boys are conditioned to cut off the signals that their bodies give them. Signals of fear may be experienced as tightness in the stomach, which is an uncomfortable sensation in the solar plexus. There may be other signals, such as sweaty palms, rapid heart rate, poor eye contact, generalized anxiety, and addictive and compulsive behaviors. Since a boy has not learned the cues and signals given by his body, he automatically dismisses the signals. He disregards his emotions; he lacks self-awareness. This process can continue into adulthood. The dismissal of emotions happens so quickly that it becomes an automatic process every time the man is experiencing a strong emotion. He learns to be a thinker, and he thinks his way through every problem. His thoughts become a way of dealing with whatever he needs to confront, leaving no room for feelings.

## Men and Fear

Our minds, without proper training, can fool us into believing we are solving our issues by thinking them through. The problem with this is that we cannot always succeed in separating our minds from our bodies. When we do succeed, we become incongruent—

our words or actions don't match our feelings. We are in denial. Professionals use the word "dysfunctional" to describe this. We are not functioning the way we are intended to function.

The boy is beginning to learn to "be in control" by avoiding the real emotional life he has inside himself. The message he learns is that he must maintain control at all costs, and he does.

Without self- knowing, without the ability to recognize his own body's signals, he is unable to perceive what others might be experiencing. He lacks this radar detector in himself and in the behavior of others. This self-detector allows us to have compassion, understanding, and acceptance of others based on how others feel. Without it, a man is unable to have that understanding (that emotional connection) with others, because he cannot do it for himself. Many men have no clue about what they feel; and they choose their actions from a predominantly fear-based and defensive response to others. It is not a connection but a reaction acted out from fear. Fear responses generate distrust in others. Fear responses are defensive, and often aggressive.

The honest truth is that when an immature man is afraid, he prepares to fight. When a boy is afraid and doesn't know he's afraid, he is not safe. His actions may be affected by the fact that he senses that he is in danger, though he is unlikely to have a clear understanding of what the danger is, or what the appropriate reaction might be. Little boys get into fights to settle a score or to prove to others, especially to their peers, that they are not "chicken." The little boy fights to prove his dominance over someone else. He protects himself by fighting. He sometimes needs to prove himself by standing in the face of danger or perceived danger, by fighting. He was taught to "fight like a man." He was taught to suck it up and do what he must do. Our culture does not teach little boys to handle their fears in any other way but through physical acts of aggression or abusive language.

We see extremes of this type of behavior in gang initiation and affiliation. Gang leaders use intimidation as a means of controlling others and maintaining power. Their soldiers are no more than little boys wanting to be men, believing that acting tough gets them to "manhood." On the contrary, it is when these men get life-time incarceration, or a life-altering experience, that they begin to shed years of fear, softening their armor. Incarceration, for some of these men, can become a life-altering experience. Unfortunately, they give up their freedom in the process. Isolation and incarceration for some of these men can create the breakdown of years of defending and protecting themselves from the emotional beatings they have experienced in their life.

## The High Rollers

On one end of the spectrum, boys who are good at playing the part that our culture has assigned to them can excel in a system that rewards them with high status, achievement, money and prestige. They are the corporate executives, lawyers, doctors, and other highly specialized professional fields (including sports) that can give men a false sense of power. These men were taught at a very early age the need to achieve and succeed, and the expectation that "successful" competitors will be rewarded. It pays to stick it out, to be tough and get the job done. This is a good thing.

What is not so good is that many of these boys become immune to their emotional selves. When that happens, they also fail to experience the "emotional payoffs" that accompany behavior we can describe as compassionate, merciful, and possibly just "fair-play." For men who become successful in their middle age years without having experienced the payoffs of "moral" and decent behavior, all hell breaks loose. The successful executive begins an affair risking his family and marriage. The sports figure suddenly gets caught using cocaine. The lawyer begins making shady deals. We might call this behavior "success at any price," for men who don't know all the meanings of success.

In recent years, men have been caught in dishonesty and deception (often referred to only as white collar crime or corruption) at Enron and Arthur Andersen and the tobacco companies that have made millions by creating addiction. These men have something in common with immature men in gangs. Both groups engage in behaviors that reveal extreme forms of dissociation from the real self. The gang banger who acts out as a tough guy, for his gang affiliation, is like the corporate executive who gets paid millions to protect people's money including his own. Both men are self serving. They are takers rather than givers. It is all about them and what they can get. These men are disconnected from the rest of society.

This corporate blindness is about men and their need to have power, even though their power is not authentic. Men with authentic power do not take advantage of others, especially those who have given them power and entrusted them to protect their interest. This self-serving mentality was trained into them. On the one hand our culture expects men to act with integrity and accountability. Integrity and accountability come from a man's sense of knowing who he is, what

he stands for. On the other hand, many of these corporate white collar men know how to play the corporate game. In so much of corporate America, it's all about beating your competition no matter what it takes and getting ahead of your competitor.

## Male Bashing

The male bashing that goes on in this country is partly justified by how men act out, reflecting a lack of accountability in their lives. Most of what people read in the media about men is negative. The "Dear Abby" columns, the magazines with advice, stories of women complaining about men and how they have been stiffed by them are all part of our culture, as though it is acceptable behavior for one person to diminish another, regardless of gender. Magazine racks are filled with relationship problem stories. Women, who are typically more expressive and in touch with their feelings, share tragic stories about their relationships with men. Men are not as eager to put their deepest disappointments in print as women appear to be. It then appears that if the men "would only get it right" somehow, then relationships would be much smoother.

On the other hand, men keep their complaints to themselves. It is not manly to complain. The label that men act like pigs is a frequently-heard expression of sentiment. Think about what a pig represents. Pigs don't have feelings. Their primary function is to roam around with their noses full of soil, feeding themselves. Pigs are selfish.

A man who does not know his own feelings is self serving. Selfishness stems from the little boy's deepest fear. Men who don't "know" their fear are unlikely to learn compassion or act from integrity. They might never have the courage to ask for what they need, because it might reveal too much of their vulnerability. It's unacceptable for them to speak a forbidden truth, by saying "I actually can't do everything alone, and I don't want to; I'm tired of feeling alone and living alone."

Each man who chooses to live in isolation is struggling to prove that a lie is actually true. The cost of the lies is the loss of being able to trust others, and the loss of feeling that it's safe to be seen, and heard and validated by others. This isolation is the loss of almost everything that makes us human, because it denies emotional experience and the joy of human companionship.

## So These are the Lies...

Too many men hear the lies without making a peep on behalf of the truth. Our silence carries the message that we agree with the lies. We lie when we don't speak out against the lies. Our silence is a lie, every bit as much standing in front of a crowd and speaking a lie.

We can begin to understand the impact of these lies in the lives of men and boys. If we don't hold ourselves to high standards of honesty as men, our lies will continue to create the model for the growth of boys that destroys emotional life and creates isolation. It's time to encourage emotional health and the adult understanding that our lives are all interrelated. We truly need each other. It's time to live in truth, together.

# Chapter 6
# The Making of a Man: The Truth...

## The Truth Begins Here.
It's simple. Our bodies tell the truth, and they don't really know how to hide it.

The exhaustion we experience during times of emotional distress is a result, at least in part, of efforts to convince the body that it's okay to ignore everything that's going on. Our bodies know the truth.

## Men and Feelings
Feelings act as a mirror, reflecting back who one is. Feelings permit a man to feel alive and connected to self and to others. Feelings function like radar, giving us signals from the heart. Heart talk is the deepest and purest level of communication. In this level of awareness, the boy inside can speak freely. We have lost this ability to speak from our hearts when our thinking process takes over.

This conditioning has withered many a man who was once a tender, innocent, loving, sensitive, fearful, joyous, dependent being. As we slowly move away from the heart-felt signals we once had as children, we move further away from the truth of ourselves. Only from the deepest level of ourselves can we know what our truth is. Speaking this truth always leads to the right path. Speaking our truth is stepping into the center of our being. It is from this place where reality can be experienced for what it truly is, rather than inventing it in our imaginations.

## The Mechanics of Feelings

Men that can access their feelings are connected to their breath. As a man breathes, he can sense his own "frame of mind" in his belly, taking his breath down to his solar plexus, and getting a reading as to what he is feeling. He breathes fully, filling up his diaphragm with breath. In this chamber, emotions are recognized or "sensed" when they are present; and they can be identified. "Am I afraid, or angry, or sad, or happy, or feeling ashamed?"

As a man senses the answer to such a question, he can speak out from his center, and know what he feels. He'll be able to trust that his words match his feelings, because he can feel it "in his gut" or "in his heart:" and others will trust that his words truly describe what he is experiencing. A man who lacks the ability to connect with this feeling in the belly can only "speak from his head" rather than from his heart or his gut. His breathing might also be shallow, from years of training this part of his body not to be a reliable indicator of his feelings, in his core, near his heart. The result is a man who speaks shallow words lacking substance and power. The lack of connection to feelings can be heard by others. Words that lack substance and power are rarely trusted by a listener. This is the situation that is often described as a relationship in which two people lack a true connection, a true "heart-to-heart" connection.

## Mirror, Mirror, on the Wall...

Can you remember an adult that inspired you? These adults inspired the dreams within us. It wasn't just that they had their dreams and felt their passions. It was that the depth of their belief was so evident and so important to them, that they taught us about that feeling of having passions of our own. They created magical moments, in which we were sustained by inspiration, passion and excitement. Can you think back to a moment when you were a child, and you remember that an adult in your life encouraged you to pursue your dream? If you see this person in your mind, do you remember the feeling you had? You probably felt free, you felt joy, and you felt powerful. You were totally engrossed in your essence of being. Your center was filled up. There was no holding back. You were in your brilliance, in your magnificence. No one was censoring your words or actions. Actually you may have marveled at what you were doing or saying.

How many of us had that experience as children, only to have it crushed by the adults around us, telling us to stop acting childish or foolish? Sometimes our joy seemed like an irritation to a parent, often resulting in a feeling of being ashamed, and wanting to hide the beautiful dream inside, where it's safe. This is one of the ways that the wound in the boy can be created. They get "bottled up." The painful moments are not released as they happen. Instead they get imprinted in the psyche of the boy as painful moments.

The boy without the capacity to feel becomes irresponsible and self centered. Self centeredness stems from a lack of proper mirroring of who one is. If a child is sad the proper adult mirror would say "You are sad." The adult would validate the inner experience of the child. Instead, the adult often denies the experience of the child; and the child turns inward with feelings that aren't released. When the feelings are denied by the adult, the child is taught to deny them as well.

69

In the Greek myth of Narcissus, Narcissus sees his own reflection in a pool, and he loves what he sees. Healthy narcissism turns into healthy self esteem. Healthy narcissism can only be provided by the validation from the adults in the boy's life. Without that spoken validation from an adult, the inexperienced boy can only see himself as he thinks he is, with the limited understanding of a child. He won't love what he sees, if he hasn't been told that the adults love what they see in him. This validation is something that a boy is almost always incapable of bringing into his life successfully. It's hard enough for the grown man.

Reflections seen by the boy, *in his limited understanding,* can lead to isolation, withdrawal and aggressive behaviors. A boy who has had the validation of adults can look in the mirror and see (or at least look for) what the adults have seen in him. And at these early ages, boys don't have the tools to "differentiate" themselves from their parents. They want to become what others want them to become. Without information from the grownups, the child does in fact become what he imagines he already is. If he has a distorted image of himself, he can carry that distorted image all the way into adulthood.

## Denial of Emotional Life

Too often, boys and young men have felt oppressed by adults and discouraged from feeling their passion, their sadness, their anger, their grief, and their joy. The full range of their emotional repertoire became fainter and fainter as they got older.

The boy needs to hear the truth about him if he is to grow into his full masculinity. The truth is that he is inherently good inside. He needs to do nothing to be loved, and to be lovable.

By the very act of his birth he has inherited a sacred trust with a power greater than any human being has, including his parents. Yet, the caregivers of this child are far from perfect, and so their own unresolved childhood may be passed on to their children through how they bring the child up. The truth is not spoken to the boy and the boy is forced through assimilation to take in what the adults say to him about who he is. All their projections and biases are spoken to him. In those childhood moments where the adult was absent, the boy is forced to fill in the gaps by creating words in his mind to fill the void of the silence. Boys don't have the internal power to believe they are loved unless they are told they are. Without that communication, they can feel unloved, and their spirits are broken.

Without any adults to validate what is naturally inside, the boy ceases to feel alive. No longer is he in command of his own world. He is driven to please, to conform, to become what others want him to become. The boy out of touch with his own feelings becomes a target for others' exploitation. As a boy, his emotions and his actions are limited to feeling and acting angry (or even rageful). These are the feelings that cut the boy off from others, especially those whom he is most dependent on. The child is unable to understand that something is terribly wrong, even when his entire set of life-choices is made up of just isolation and anger. Without the other emotions, he will have nothing but isolation in his life, created and perpetuated by his anger at being alone.

## Emotions are Key

Research strongly suggests that emotions in humans are based on our genetic makeup. They are part of what makes us human, and they're the basis for our need to be connected with one another. Feelings allow a man to identify with others, have compassion for others, and have the capacity to imagine being (as they say) in the other person's shoes. Feelings are like fuel. Feelings fuel a man's path toward positive outcomes in his world.

Feelings are the music of the soul. The chamber of the soul is the heart. In the heart we experience living. Memories are stored in the mind, but it is in our hearts that we set ourselves free. Once a man feels safe enough to begin internally communicating with his inner boy, he begins to express his tender self that he has lost early on.

When a man begins to get in touch with his inner boy, he feels lighter for the first time. As the inner boy begins to speak up for the first time, he is frightened, not knowing that his truth will be heard. He does not know that his feelings are his truth. This is the time in which the boy hears a louder voice. He is confused, and he doesn't trust what he speaks. He hears instead the voices from others. Others have told him to be brave, to be strong, to shut up, to stop crying, to stuff it. On and on, words that are not his own play in his head.

But growth begins with a change. This time is different; this time he begins to hear what he has not heard before; and it's his own voice. The emotions can be overwhelming. There is a mixture of relief and fear. He needs to trust his own voice that comes from his deep well-- a well that is filled up.

As the inner boy speaks more of his truth, he develops confidence that this is his own voice. He is the one now in charge. The voices of others slowly begin to be whispers, and as time passes they become even fainter. In the end, the truth is his now, his to be spoken. He knows it and feels empowered for the first time.

The shift from feeling "locked up" inside to feeling freedom can be overwhelming at times. Not knowing if this is alright to feel, many need encouragement at this time. From withholding to letting go, the early imprints begin to be challenged by the new feelings of well being inside. This is the beginning of emotional growth.

## So This is Still the Truth

The lies have such strength that they can only be overcome by enormous authenticity and honesty from men as a group, to create new standards of behavior that replace the old standards, which simply repeat the lies.

Without the capacity to look inside and see himself as he truly is, the immature man sometimes chooses to live "for others" and not for himself. He would still be an approval seeker. Just like a child, his actions would be guided so that they get approval from others, primarily from the ones whom he cherishes most in his life.

Even though there is some evidence to suggest that men's perceptions of themselves are slowly changing, our culture has a long way to go for the most part as it continues to socialize men to value things over people. Men have trouble distinguishing between things and people, as sources of satisfaction in their lives. Sometimes they also treat people as though they're just objects. When a couple seeks treatment, women often complain that their husbands are selfish and think little of others. He puts himself first. Consequently the burden of the family is on her shoulders.

For many men the paycheck still provides the identity. As long as the man provides for the family, he feels he has met his responsibility. He feels he is doing what a man is supposed to do. This is a myth of the man that was handed down, and it includes all these views of the world: A man's job is to work for his family and provide for them. The time a man spends with his family is not quality time. They (the family) don't see him for what he truly is. A man is entitled to feel he has done his job with family, as long as he provides for them and he works hard for them. When he comes home, he wants to be treated as a prince and be waited on and served, because he finished his day's work before going home. He feels that home is a place where there's no work to do, and no responsibility.

What such a man fails to understand is that what his family really needs is not his paycheck, but his time. What the family often gets from the man instead is his anger and his temper.

This continues to be true: The cycle of family breakdown continues from one generation to the next. Children don't get the time they need from their fathers, and they re-create a similar scenario when they reach adulthood. When we continue to live as though we can deny our feelings as humans, we create havoc in the world. This will continue to be true, until we change it.

The good news is that we can change the world, through the actions we take in our lives. Change in one man can be fast, if the man is ready. Change in a culture will take time. We'd better get started right now.

# Chapter 7
# Men and Power

If you were asked about your understanding of "feeling loved" and "feeling powerful," how would you describe those two things? Do you recognize or remember yourself as having a strong need to feel loved? Do you feel almost helpless at times, almost powerless to do something that you want (or need) to do? Is there a connection between feeling loved and feeling powerful in your life, or do they seem entirely different and separate?

Your answers might reveal your earliest understandings about relationships, as well as the learning you've gained from relationships as you've grown.

As children, each of us was unable to understand the meaning of concepts like love and power. Even as grownups, we know that there are many many ways to understand these concepts. It's difficult to talk about these concepts meaningfully without having a shared understanding, so I'll tell you what I believe is true as a starting place.

My understanding of the relationship between love and power in a person's life seems simple. The capacity for feeling loved comes from inside. The actual feeling of being loved is the feeling of joy that comes from sharing a close relationship, in which two people choose to give one another what they want or need, in order to be happy together. Personal power is the acceptance that my own life is the only place in which I have any power at all, and it's only in my own life that I can have real impact. Personal power includes a deep understanding of personal responsibility, in the knowledge that I'm the only one who will ever truly be responsible for my happiness. I'm the only one who has the power to make me happy, through my choices and my willingness to ask for what I want. I can choose to give others what they want or need in order to be happy, and I know that I'll feel the happiness that I can share with them in that way.

I tell you these things because I've worked with many men who have changed their understanding of these things in the course of therapy, and they tell me that they never knew what they were missing. Maybe the patterns in their lives will have meaning for you.

Many men have been taught (or taught themselves) that gaining more and more material things is a way to increase a man's sense of personal power, and that this will be a source of happiness in life. They look outside themselves for a source of "feeling good," instead of looking inside.

Even though these men may acquire more and more of the "stuff" that can be seen as a collection of "trophies," they may also continue to deny or ignore the feelings that they could experience. They can continue to feel isolated and unloved, even if they have relationships. They continue to look for happiness outside themselves, expecting that someday their partners will figure out how to give them what they need but can't give themselves. Relationships like that don't work. The people who care for these men usually recognize this isolation, and they know that they can't make it go away. In these ways, men hurt themselves and their relationships with others.

A man's identity isn't based on his job or the property he owns; that's a lie. A man's true identity is based on his sense of self, and not on what he does or has. This distinction is important. A man who believes the old lie values achievement and results above all. His emphasis is on how many badges and trophies he can display for others to see. For him, a man's identity is his job, his money, his possessions, his toys. All that he collects is to increase his status and prestige, to get recognition from others. A man is socialized to compete and conquer. It's about winning and not losing. It's about showmanship. He stands alone on the podium to show others (including other men) that he is on top. His primary purpose is to win over others, to be better than others, and to control others for his own ego inflation.

A man with a true sense of self knows that there is more value in his life than just the items he has accumulated and the accomplishments he has achieved. He knows that the value in his life is in his relationships.

Real power doesn't come from the outside. It comes from within. Real power is the combination of having a man's actions match his feelings, and of knowing the value of relationships in his life. A powerful man doesn't choose to live his life alone. His connection to the world is relationship-based. The idea that he lives in relationship with others (and that his welfare is dependent on others) is a point of view that he may never have been taught in his early upbringing. He may also have learned this lesson at a young age, or reinforced it as an adult. A man without relationships can't experience the powerful pleasure of having a "full" life.

Many men are less in tune with cause and effect in relationships than most women (and other men) are. Since they have been taught to be selfish and to think that they are so independent that they have no connections with others, men are often not in touch with how their actions affect others. In this incomplete interaction with the world, interpersonal relationships are absent from the personal experiences of many men, because they were not socialized to be considerate and compassionate. Instead they are taught to perform, to win, and to play at being the "macho man."

In this world, a man having a sensitive heart might be viewed as weak or wimpy. His sensitivity might also be so unfamiliar to some men that they react in a way that reveals their fears about what it means to be "manly." Those men might also fear that sensitive hearts in the community would teach boys to have "softer" ways that they may not have experienced, and might send young men along the path of being gay/homosexual.

Instead, mature men know that another man's choices mean nothing in their own lives (unless it's a choice of whether to have a strong relationship with another person).

Men who lack the experiences of consideration and compassion haven't been shown the full range of responses that are possible in the world; and they continue to see the world with eyes that see only the things they are accustomed to seeing. They are both blind and powerless. Until they can see that the strongest men have the deepest and the most powerful relationships, with both men and women, these men will have lives that lack joy and the feeling of power that relationships bring, as the greatest source of joy in a man's life.

## Maintaining the Image

Men have a very difficult time with the concept of "being." They know about doing, but they don't know about being. Men often lack the "mirror" that they need, made up of information that others (the "grownups") have given them, to understand what they are feeling and showing to the world. A big part of "being" is just "feeling and not doing." This is why so many men can easily tell you what they do, while lacking the knowledge of what kind of man they are. If you ask such men "What kind of man are you," many will answer by telling you what they do. They don't connect with a sense of their "being" because that connection requires that a man experience his feelings.

Extensive television coverage followed a series of sniper shootings in the metropolitan Washington D.C. area. On October 7, 2002, after the shooting death of a 13-year-old boy, Montgomery County Police Chief Charles Moose spoke of that death on live television. As he spoke, he began to shed tears in front of millions of viewers. He was showing his love for humanity and his sadness over the senseless loss of life, his pain, and the connection he felt with this child and the people who loved him. He was showing his humanity as an authentic man, and many viewers didn't like what they saw. Here was a leader in a position of power showing real emotions.

He wasn't playing the part in the make-believe world of cops and robbers. This wasn't The Lone Ranger. He wasn't reading from a script. These shootings actually affected him personally. Yet, many viewers wanted and expected him to feel no pain. They wanted him to act out the myth that men don't cry, especially not in front of others- and even more so if the man they see is in a position of influence or power.

The truth is that he was a powerful man in a powerful position showing the real power of a man who feels connected with other human beings. In front of millions, he let men see how powerful a man can be, in a flash. In front of millions, he broke the myths and fallacies of power, and most of all, of men in power.

Our culture perpetuates the falsehood that it's okay for strong men to feel pain, so long as they never show their pain in front of others. It encourages men to deny something that is actually true—to deny that they're feeling pain. This denial is nonsense; and it's dangerous and unhealthy behavior if we are going to become a more humane world.

Which man would you trust more, the man who is actually feeling pain while communicating that he isn't feeling pain or the man who is feeling pain and letting it show? Why is it acceptable for our culture to expect men to lie to one another, so that a lie can be acted out? It's not acceptable. The police chief demonstrated leadership as a man who has a sense of his "being," his feelings. He demonstrated true bravery and true authenticity by letting television viewers see the feelings that he was experiencing. It takes a strong man to step into his authenticity and show his true self.

## Solid as a Rock
Another part of the "Male Myth" is that vulnerability is a sign of weakness, and being strong means not being vulnerable.

Being vulnerable is having the capacity to experience feelings, instead of denying that feelings are happening. When a person attempts to deny or ignore the powerful energy of big feelings, that energy doesn't just go away; it stays in the person as stress; and stress is damaging to a person's health. One of the reasons women live longer than men is that they cope better than men in times of stress, by expressing themselves more fully during critical times. Women are permitted to feel and fully express their emotions. Their coping mechanisms (having their feelings) are very well integrated, compared to the coping mechanisms of men. Women during stressful events can experience fear, hurt, sadness, loss. Men, for the most part, stuff these feelings deeper and deeper into themselves, and then begin their denial that the feelings ever happened to them.

Soon these men begin denying that they're experiencing stress, too, because most men lack a coping mechanism that works better than denial. This ineffective coping behavior isn't a sign of being vulnerable, and it isn't a sign of mature male strength, and statistically it causes men to die at earlier ages than women. The part of the Male Myth that says vulnerability is a sign of weakness is simply untrue. Being vulnerable is a sign of true emotional health and mature male strength.

Stress is the result of being unable (or unwilling) to deal with emotions effectively. Men tend to isolate and disconnect from others during stressful times. A man may have a flood of feelings; but in place of learning to process feelings effectively, he may have learned to withdraw from contact before he is overwhelmed by the feelings he doesn't want to experience. All his efforts to avoid being overwhelmed lead him to withdraw from others. In a way, what he may need the most he doesn't get-- support from the people he cares about the most. He may disconnect from his family, or be more preoccupied and distracted at work; and the most he can do is "ride out the storm."

The strong will that permits a man to ride out the storm seems like a virtue; and it is a virtue if the man is willing to find a new approach when the old ways aren't working. But staying with the same unsuccessful approach to a problem only increases the stress in a man's life. Studies show that men suffer from more stress-related disease than women do. There is a direct correlation between disease and emotions. Even though stress has become a "buzz-word," the reality is that stress shortens a man's life.

Healthy men make choices that reduce the stress in their lives, and in the world. An unhealthy man's way of "coping" may become aggressive behavior, and even acts of violence, in an effort to experience some feeling that resembles being alive. Aggression and violence are rampant in our culture now, as they have been throughout history. Violent men create a violent world. Every man who is unable to show up fully as a human being creates consequences in the world, similar to a disease that spreads without stopping. These consequences touch every part of the world, affecting not only the man who lacks humanity, but also everyone else whose life he touches.

## The Broken Boy—The Boy without a Mentor

Being broken is the same as being disconnected from a trusted source of feedback about the "boy's" place in the world. It might mean that the boy is totally isolated and alone. It might mean that he has no "higher authority." It might mean that he has a life with such chaos that the grownups can't be trusted—and the boy can only do the best he can do, with the goal of just surviving until he's older.

What does a boy know about male power? A boy's idea of power comes from what he has been taught (or has taught himself) about the adult world. The teaching comes from different sources-- his caretakers, his everyday surroundings, and what he sees his peers doing. He gets constant reinforcement of what is and isn't power. His mind is open to influence.

There is no filtering of what is good for him, and what is bad. He takes it all in without the ability to judge it from a mature, healthy understanding of the world. He is a boy wanting to become a man. He learns that power is something to get, to take, to win, to take over, to achieve, to finish, to perform, or to make. Power is something that is obtained from the world outside of him, rather than a quality that he carries inside, where it's always with him. A boy may not have felt empowered to see that choice in his view of the world.

For the most part, boys are not mentored in a process of developing this type of personal power, of making "good" choices, based on what they know and trust to be true. It's only when the growing boy feels empowered to choose that he can recognize his own feeling of power in his life.

In this culture, boys who don't receive mentoring from a man with a mature male's understanding of power will invent an understanding of power based on everything they hear and see, including all of the negative, unhealthy views of male power. He will probably be encouraged to push towards something, perhaps a goal and a plan. The boy wants to please. He needs the adults. He needs their admiration to keep pushing himself forward toward adulthood. He will do whatever it takes to get the admiration of the adult. In most cases he seeks admiration from his caretakers, his parents.

The conditioning of the boy happens in all cultures in all ethnic communities. No boy is spared. Boys instinctually know what is expected of them at a very early age. The need for love is the most powerful need we have. Early feelings of "being loved" are frequently connected with behavior that has pleased the caretaker. The more the caretaker seems pleased, the more the boy senses that his choices are "right" or "good," because his choices are met with an approving response from the people who are most important in his life.

Because boys are starving for the attention of men who will guide them on a growth process, many young men are harmed by the choices they make. To the young boy who hasn't connected with a mature male's way of giving support and encouragement, even the attention of "corrupt mentors" will become desirable, possibly in the form of gang leaders and religious extremists and others who will exploit the isolation and denial of feelings that they find in the immature male. Their leadership usually harms the young men that they attract, sometimes leaving permanent emotional damage and sometimes killing the young men who make the wrong choice of a "mentor" in their lives.

Boys whose families are dysfunctional and full of conflict, where there is a high level of stress and family life is chaotic and unpredictable, are likely to become their own immature mentors, when they decide to repress their authenticity for the sake of survival. They may have experienced constant yelling and screaming between parents, or repeatedly seeing a father drunk and abusive. They may have taken the emotional or physical blows from tyrannical fathers, or they may have been hurt by their peers for the petty reasons of children. They may have been abandoned emotionally (or even physically) by father or mother or both. In a highly abusive family relationship, the boy begins to cut off from his feelings and from his caretakers. He develops adaptive ways to cope that serve him well during that period by reducing his experience of the abuse and the conflict as much as he possibly can.

When he becomes an adult, though, the coping mechanisms he invented as a child have stopped working in his favor. In fact, the coping mechanism of isolation that was his friend as a child begins to be an adversary that works against him. By choosing isolation or denial of his feelings, he continues to live his life as though his unpredictable and chaotic life is still present. The feelings that were not encouraged (or not safe to express) create a feeling of intolerable stress, like an explosion that is about to happen. So some men increase their denial of what they're feeling again, until they can't quite feel anything that's going on in their bodies. This willingness to go through life feeling nothing takes on different forms, including emotional disorders that require the help of mental health professionals. One familiar response to this intolerable stress is the "fight or flight" response that we can experience in moments of extreme fear, when we have to choose whether to "stand and fight" or "run like hell." A man whose life is filled with stress is a man who never learned the coping strategies of mature males.

What makes a man "broken" is that he still has no safe emotional place. He might not recognize such a place, and he certainly can't create one. If he has no safe emotional place to be authentic and feel stressful experiences, he disconnects from his emotional response. He does this as though he can bring himself comfort by simply deciding to ignore his discomfort. That decision can never be more than partially successful. The cost of that decision to ignore emotional discomfort is often the experience of distress, which is even far more uncomfortable.

Distress starts building inside the man, like a feeling of being surrounded by chaos. There is no place for him to identify and express what he feels inside. He does not have any adults who can mirror his distress back and validate his internal experience. He is totally on his own. Without any encouragement or guidance, the boy becomes "broken" inside. Everything begins to feel disconnected.

What he is thinking and what he is feeling become scrambled. His connection between his external and internal world is cut off. He sees the chaos outside himself, but because there is no place for his internal feelings, his body starts to tense up. His stomach is in knots or he has sweaty palms, or nightmares, or he starts to get angrier in school, or becomes more quiet and reclusive at home. He gets very hyper and "wired," unable to slow down or calm himself from his experience of terrible stress, and he has no way to soothe himself. After hundreds (or thousands) of moments like these throughout the lifetime of this boy growing toward adulthood, the result is a tight, repressed, denied and troubled boy (or man).

Men are powerful beings. Power does not come in the form of brute strength, but it comes in the form of vulnerability to emotion. Men's work is about giving up the childhood lies about what makes a man, through relentless self-examination, active integration and self-awareness. Self-awareness is a result of the immediate feedback a man is receiving from his entire being—the feelings that he can recognize in his body. With his feelings, he learns what he needs for himself and from others. He learns that his needs are the cornerstone of his life. In learning about his needs, he becomes more responsible for meeting his own needs. With that new understanding, he can begin to serve himself and others.

## Growth Hurts

Distress is a state of agitation. Men in distress can't comfort themselves. The energy present in agitation fuels men into physical and emotional symptoms that can also take the form of inappropriate behavior. It's a disconnection from the emotional "self." Reconnecting with the true emotional self is the only way to live authentically. It takes the determination of a grown man to do the growth that was somehow skipped or missed. That growth will almost always be a painful experience.

It will be necessary for a man to feel the original pain of a painful experience, in order to experience it fully, and re-interpret his responses to that experience in a new way.

## On Feelings and Distress

Feelings are the pathways that lead a man to be a fully integrated man, whose actions are congruent with what he's feeling. The first time a man begins to identify his feelings there is a burst of energy and freedom. He's out of the cage. He doesn't feel constricted or tense. His somatic complaints (the physical and emotional symptoms that result from distress) lessen. He can channel his feelings naturally without somatisizing them.

Men that we describe as integrated in this way have the ability to choose to experience their feelings and give them their proper honor, without hiding from them. Men who lack this ability lead lives of high stress, sometimes with such a high sense of chaos that they feel panic attacks and true physical symptoms, as their bodies attempt to address the apparent danger that is signaled by extreme stress.

## Addictions and Feelings

When I talk about addictions, I am using the word to mean not only all those addictions that are physically addicting such as alcohol and drugs, but also any habitual pattern of thought and behavior that a person has and is unable to control. In other words, an addiction is any persistent, obsessive thought that takes a man away from his real feelings, and leads toward compulsive acts.

Addiction is a temporary fix, a way to escape your reality at the moment by cutting yourself off. This can take the form of gambling, eating, sex, alcohol and drugs, shopping, or working. For whatever reason, there is less "social disapproval" of other forms of obsessive behavior, including excessive television viewing, use of the internet, and endlessly watching sports. There are other forms of addiction that I haven't named.

What these behaviors have in common is that men (and women) indulge in these behaviors to avoid their life issues. When the addiction is active, a man's actions are clouded and he is misguided by an impulse that he doesn't control. It's the addictive act that controls him every time. He is a slave to it, and until he gives up acting out his compulsive behavior, he will not know what he feels. Research studies have shown that chemicals are released that produce euphoric feelings when individuals are active in their addictive patterns, similar to the use of drugs, even when there are no drugs or alcohol in the addictive pattern.

Addiction is a disconnection that masquerades as a connection. It's a "connection" that can't serve the man, because it disconnects from the world that is real, in order to connect to a world that isn't real.

In all addictions one thing is common, and that is in the denial that the addictive act has more control over the person than the person is willing to admit. No one wants to admit they have no control over something. It can feel shameful not to be in control. Yet, that is the truth of this reality. The man doesn't admit he has a problem. When he is in denial, he does not know he is harming (even destroying) himself; and he doesn't know how he is affecting those around him.

He takes no responsibility whatsoever and blames others. When confronted, he will do everything else but acknowledge the obvious. His inflated ego is untouchable and impenetrable. Those around him suffer by his addiction, because he has no capacity for human contact that can make a difference. The addict may finally give up his delusion that he is okay when he is stuck in the middle of the tracks, and he knows a train is going to hit him, and there is no way out. When he admits and accepts that he is powerless, he can accept the help that he may have needed for years.

A man who is active in his addiction cannot access his full masculinity. Men in active addictions are emotionally immature. They stay small, hiding and denying their real feelings, escaping discomfort, and lacking will power.

There are many men who do struggle to experience their feelings, without turning to addictions as a vicarious way to get his needs met. And certainly, there are men who have no addictive lifestyle yet are emotionally dead inside. A man can also have an addiction and experience a wide range of feelings. The keys to masculine emotional health are the integration of a willingness to experience feelings, with the power to make choices and understand personal responsibility.

An authentic man has the capacity to feel and to make choices. He knows his limitations and his liabilities, and knows how to seek what he needs. An addictive man who is in a recovery process is learning that what he used to do is self destructive and ultimately futile.

A man in recovery also has learned that what he really needed and was starved for was not his addiction, but a very profound hunger for feeling "filled" in a spiritual way. A man in recovery has the understanding that his addiction was a hunger for a connection with his divine spirit. He understands that his addiction will never be satisfied by his obsessive-compulsive behavior. The more he does it, the more he wants it. The more he wants it, the more he thinks about it. It is a vicious, self-defeating cycle. Only in recovery does he come to realize this. Addictive men without any recovery have no choice, living only for their addiction. Without an authentic sense of "self" a man will not be able to heal himself, or help heal the wounds in others that have passed from one generation to the next.

When a man begins his recovery, he starts the long process of waking up. He leaves the fog and the storms, and the highs of euphoria and the lows of a bottomless abyss, and he gets a sense of grounding. Eventually, after the physical and psychological withdrawals of his addiction, he begins to see himself as he is in a recovery program. What is he now? He is a man in recovery who has chosen to admit he has a problem. This choice of admission can save his life and begin a new one. Recovery is not about achievement. It is a process of healing. Healing is a life process. It has no end. In recovery, a man learns about his feelings. He learns he has them. He learns to identify what they are, takes ownership, and learns to express the true nature of his being for the first time.

The mask is taken off and the authentic self is seen. A man can cry, be joyful, and all in between. He is no longer within any norms or standards of conduct other than his own experience of himself. He is himself no matter what he is doing. He learns to be authentic for the first time, giving up the false personas that he needed, to act out in the world.

A man knows when he is becoming authentic. It feels right inside. It feels that what he speaks and what he does are extensions of his truth. When a man learns about his authenticity, he knows when he is not authentic. He can now choose to either play the part, or be himself. When a man does not know his own feelings, he has no choice but to play the part of what others want him to be. He does not know what he needs until he feels.

## The Problem for Boys

No matter what it is like for the boy growing up, his feelings will be compromised. Expected to conform to the adult expectations, his survival instincts will kick in and he will begin repressing his authentic self to get the approval he needs from the adults in his life.

As children we enter the world of adults. We are vulnerable creatures needing to survive. This is our dilemma. We are totally dependent for every need we have. This is a biological fact. This very fact spearheads the issue for boys. By nature children are dependent on adults for their survival. This dependency supersedes the need to be authentic. Children instinctually know they need the adult in order to survive, and they will do whatever it takes to assure this survival.

Adding to this dependency, at a very early age, perhaps even at a preverbal level, boys are socialized to disown what they feel. This socialization is very unconscious on the parts of our caretakers and passed on from one generation to the next. At a very early age, boys are expected to feel less than girls, and to be less emotional than girls. Studies have also shown that boys are biologically wired differently than girls. Brain scans that can measure brain activity illustrate that boys have less chemical activity at the section of the brain that is responsible for language and expression. Boys are much more aggressive than girls; and studies have shown that boys prefer aggressive play more than girls do. Boys are not taught that they will have emotional needs. The reality is we do have these needs.

## Pleasing the Parent

The need to please the caretaker for survival during the early years of life develops instinctually. The boy will be all that his parents want him to be. He will be whatever he has to be, in order to survive.

The boy encounters an obstacle in his path at some point. He might say: "If I am dependent on you for my survival, then I must know what it is that you want me to do so that I can get what I need. Even so, I may give you what you want, but it may or it may not give me what I need." The boy's challenge is survival, self-preservation.

"And if your needs are stronger than mine, I will die." This "dying" is that the child will no longer be the same person after realizing that his own needs might be hidden or denied in his struggle for survival. We call this several names-- stuffing, shoving, pushing aside, repressing, and hiding our feelings. This is the beginning of stress in the life of the boy.

## What Mature Men Need

A man needs to know what others really think of him. He doesn't need to hear what others think he wants to hear. He needs to hear what is true for us as we speak to him, without tainting it or sugar coating it. A man often needs to hear truth from another man even more than from a woman. Most men have difficulty trusting others, because they've been taught to be self-reliant and independent from a very early age. Do young men hear that they should trust others? "Handle things on your own, don't trust anybody but yourself. Men do it alone." These are powerful messages that contribute to a man's lack of trust in others. A mature man needs to have trust in himself and in others, in order to thrive. Without that trust, even a grown man has no safe place.

## Men as Partners

If you're in a committed relationship with another person, whether legally or by agreement, and you're struggling to make it work, you may be looking for help with conflict. If you're not looking at how you contribute to this conflict, you're only seeing part of the picture. If you want conflict to go away, you need to understand that it won't go away by somebody else doing all the work of removing the conflict. As we grow into mature men, we realize that we have responsibilities. Until a man accepts his responsibilities (especially in relationships), he fits the description of a "wannabe." He wants to be a man, but he isn't. This "label" may fit an experience you're having in a relationship. I use this label to identify emphatically that a man who has not reached maturity in relationships will sometimes deny his accountability in the relationship with his partner, by believing or by claiming that he isn't responsible for the problem.

When a man does not take ownership for what he does and says, we might say he is acting boyish; he's acting like a "wannabe man." As mentioned earlier in this book, a boy or young man doesn't understand how to take or accept responsibility for his feelings. He hasn't been taught to feel, and instead he disconnects from his feelings. If he can't experience his own feelings, he can't understand the feelings of his relationship partner. Disconnection from feelings in a relationship is an immature man's attempt to isolate himself from responsibility for his contribution to the conflict with his partner. Acceptance of that responsibility is the first step toward nurturing and increasing the intimacy you are having with your partner.

Accountability is the acceptance of responsibility. Most of the men I work with start with a lack of accountability in their intimate relationships. They feel they have no control in this relationship. They feel beaten down and blame their partner for how they are feeling. Blame is unwillingness to be held accountable. Blaming your partner takes away your power. It also doesn't give you what you need to get it back on track. Blame is never the answer for a lack of closeness with your partner. If you give blame, you will get blame back. If you are defensive, you will get defensiveness back.

Whatever you put into your relationship, you will get it back. That is the law of human relationships. No more and no less.

Since relationships demand growth, you can be sure that repairing a relationship will involve painful feelings. This is the moment when a mentor should tell you that it's time to choose between living as a grown man, or continuing to live as a boy. You can choose to continue living as you are now, with distress and other forms of pain. Or you can choose the pain of growing into a mature man who accepts his responsibility for everything that "happens to him." Your mentor should also challenge you: "Are you willing to do whatever it takes to make that happen? This isn't about doing; this is about changing your way of being."

**If you are asking right now "Do you mean that this is all up to me?" then you need to know that the answer is "Yes, it's all up to you." Are you ready to make that choice?**

Before you can repair the relationship you must come to terms with the fact that you are in pain, not getting your needs met. Ultimately, you are the only one responsible for whether your needs are met. Your partner can help you meet those needs if you communicate them as very clear messages from you about your needs, wants and desires. Stress and conflict are created when one partner needs something but feels a sense of helplessness about it, especially if he reacts by blaming the other partner (and abandoning the partnership). It's far better to recognize and accept (and then communicate) those feelings of helplessness to your partner. In a loving partnership, there isn't abandoning or blaming when a partner feels fearful or helpless, even when the outcome of a problem seems totally outside the couple's control.

98

To begin the change from being a wannabe man to being a healthy partner with your significant other, ask yourself this question: What are you putting into this relationship, and what are you getting back? Anger and accusations can be signs that you are not taking responsibility for your feelings. Anger that is never resolved is a sign that the person who is angry is avoiding responsibility for his (or her) half of the problem. If you're angry about someone else's actions, you need to express in a grown way how it is affecting you, without blaming or shaming. For example, you might say: " I'm angry that you spend this much money without discussing it with me; I feel neglected, as though you don't care about what I think or need, and I feel all alone when you spend money we don't have."

Here, you've expressed how you felt, and provided valuable information to your partner. You've laid the groundwork for open discussion, without blame. You've communicated a message that speaks about how you feel, without name-calling or blaming. When we speak about ourselves, the person we're speaking to usually feels less defensive and can allow honest feelings to emerge in response. In communication between two partners, both people are permitted to speak and to be heard.

The first goal is to hear one another. The second goal is to know what the other person is feeling. These two statements are true of communications in all relationships, whether they are based on romance or friendship or business.

## Men as Fathers

When a man becomes a biological or a psychological father, he has new responsibilities. A mature man who has reclaimed his masculinity knows instinctually the feeling of having become "a life-giver," a participant in the creation of a new life. He understands the power of this fact in his life, and has a deep appreciation for the responsibility he has in shaping his child's view of himself and others. He takes the relationship as a sacred act of creation, and can choose to place himself in partnership with his creator to shape the child's life. This is truly a humbling experience for men who see themselves as sacred beings. Even without a connection to sacred consciousness, men can experience fathering as profoundly satisfying.

Mature masculine fathering is a sacred act of love, a long series of loving gifts to a man's children. A man who has not fully matured and stays emotionally boy-like will not be able to step up to the bat to assure that his children develop healthy internal mechanisms for dealing with life's challenges. The internal hardware includes a well developed sense of self, so that the children may feel they are loved and are capable and worthy of receiving love.

It's in the energy of the father, by his example, that the boy learns to accept his softer and vulnerable self. The father's way of being becomes the model for the boy. The boy gets the message that being emotionally authentic is being a real man.

A man who is on a healing path can distinguish between the type of fathering that benefits his children or harms them emotionally. An effective parent can accept that he's imperfect and will make mistakes in parenting his children, but he knows he has a great deal to contribute to the overall welfare of his children. He encourages them to have good feelings about themselves, and is able to nurture his children physically and emotionally. He is able to be in partnership with his children, and can understand subtle changes in their feelings, so that he can make the constant changes that a parent needs to make to adapt to the needs of the children. He can validate the feelings of the child as they happen, instead of encouraging the denial of feelings. He can apologize when he makes mistakes, demonstrating that he's human and showing consideration and respect for his children, and demonstrating that a grown man can make mistakes and admit them. If the father demonstrates compassion and kindness and regret, the children are more likely to adopt the same behaviors.

It's true that actions speak louder than words. A father's teaching can be more powerful in his actions that his words. He teaches his children all the time by his actions, how he treats his relationships with his family members, his partner, his own children, and others who are closest to him. The best gift a father can give a child is his loving presence, and the opportunity to see the father as a mature and authentic man.

Too many times I've seen the consequences of the double standard that exists between the father and the child in the statement "Do as I say, not as I do." Too often there's a father making that statement who is unwilling to be seen as an authentic man, and unwilling to accept responsibility for giving advice that he doesn't accept as guidance in his own life. Those words reflect the man's willingness to remain disconnected and powerless in his own life, and the children who hear this often incorporate the same behavior into their own lives. It's another form of isolation and abandonment.

When I talk with children and adults that have had the benefit of getting psychological help from professionals, they often say that as children they had low self-esteem, and they felt that their fathers "weren't there for them" emotionally. These statements describe fathers who, in their words and actions, created more harm than good. When these children describe the relationships they had with their parents, they almost always say that they didn't feel loved and wanted.

The words of a friend of mine sound like good advice to all the fathers, so that their children don't grow up feeling alone and unloved. He says: "Live your life knowing that when you were born, you cried and the world was full of joy, and when you die, the world will cry, and you can be full of joy."

Make a difference in the world. Don't miss the opportunity to transform your child's life by the example you give in how you choose to live your own life. Grown men don't just want to pass through this world. They care about the legacy they leave behind.

# Chapter 8
# A Conversation with the Reader

## Note to the Reader

*For every journey, we need to know what to expect. Getting started on a journey requires preparation. On this trip, there isn't a map that will lead you directly to a destination, because you don't know at all where you're going. How do you prepare for such a journey?*

*Even if you already have a close and trusted friend that you might ask for directions on the road to mature male growth, I want to speak to you like a close friend who has experienced some of the difficulties you're about to face. If you're asking why I might want to do that, I'll tell you simply that I care about your growth, and I want you to succeed in becoming the man that you can become. Your growth is important to me because I believe that our world needs every man who is willing to learn a new way to live, so that his relationships are stronger with the men and the women and the children and the principles that guide his life. I don't know for certain what you are experiencing in your life right now, but I know a few things about what you might experience along this "path" toward growth. And I want you to know those things, so that you can be prepared to start.*

*There are so many true statements I can offer about this journey, because they've been proven by the experiences of many men. I write them here because you may have doubts about whether to take the first step. You may doubt yourself as seriously as that. You may also get discouraged along the way if progress isn't as fast as you think* it "should" be. So, before I give you examples of the ways that you may feel doubt about your courage for completing the trip, I want you to read these few brief statements, because they're true, and a time may come when you can remember them just before proving that they are also true for you.

Read these four statements below, and remember them on your journey.

It's never too late for a man to begin or continue his growth process.

It will be scary sometimes. We human beings find it extraordinarily difficult to change. You are almost certain to feel fear, when you think about the changes you will make in your life.

You can still be the man you always wanted to be, even if you can't guess right now what that will feel like to you. You'll learn along the way.

I believe in you, and in your power to accomplish huge changes in your life. I know you can do it.

The remainder of this chapter is provided to you as a set of examples and explanations, so that you know that other men have experienced the same things that you may experience on your journey. When you notice that you've started waking up most mornings knowing that you respect the actions you choose to take, then you'll probably experience the feeling of "liking" the man that you have become. If you've never experienced that feeling before, you will be learning one *of the ways in which mature men experience joy in their lives. My wish for you is that you begin to create that joy, so that you might feel it every day of your life. You can do that. Don't wait for a "sign" that you're ready to begin this journey. You're ready now, or you wouldn't be reading this. You started your journey long ago. Your conscious journey starts now.*

*Blessings on your Journey,*

*Alberto*

## The Journey Begins— The Battle within Yourself

Someday you'll look back and realize you're one of the men who knows the truth of the statements that you're about to read. You'll know that there are no shortcuts on the journey to healthy masculine maturity. There are no free rides. It's just plain hard. This path is chosen daily, and there's only one choice: Stay connected with what you can feel to be real inside you, and stay "in truth" in all your moments, never engaging in denial that you're having feelings, and always feeling them instead, and naming them for what they are: Joy, Sadness, Anger, Fear and Shame.

These are choices that we must make over and over again, in order to know what we are feeling, and to be honest with ourselves and with others about what we are experiencing. Each such choice requires having the courage to feel the truth inside, to own it, and to share it if you choose. Know that these words sound easy, and represent choices that can be very difficult. Each choice is a step in the direction of "increasing maturity" that a man makes as he moves forward, by taking one step at a time. Because the mature man's goal is for his maturity always to be increasing, this journey never ends. The destination is always in the future.

Along the way, there are many rites of passage in the movement from childhood to adulthood. Each of these "initiation rituals" is an event that can be experienced as validation of internal changes that are about to take place, or may already have occurred. Initiation events provide feedback to the growing boy, from the grownups. They are affirmations that his growth is worthy of approval. The young man sometimes receives substantial new rights or privileges by participating in or completing a ritual process. And sometimes the recognition simply affirms that he is taking good steps in his growth process.

Remember that the young man wants to please others, and his needs can only be met if they are met immediately. As the boy grows, he learns to evaluate the positive feedback he receives in order to guide his future actions (not just things that happen immediately), so that he can produce even more approval in his life. Gradually these moments of recognition also teach the young man that he can choose his actions to create "significance" in his life, as he experiences the feelings of pride and satisfaction that mature men feel as they learn about "right" and "wrong" and other higher ways of evaluating behavior.

When a man chooses his actions from a place that reflects his own higher state of consciousness, he begins to listen even more closely to the feedback he gets from his feelings. He can see himself as having many dimensions in his personality. He experiences the world in more ways, and he knows that there is much more "reality" than he can experience with just his five senses of touching, tasting, smelling, hearing, and seeing.

Mature men and women take the "higher ground" on principle, rather than simply to pursue pleasure or to avoid pain. They've learned to recognize the feeling of conflict that they experience when they know that they want something that will benefit themselves, but might have negative consequences for other people that they care about. They're also willing to give up immediate gratification in order to have the greater satisfaction of knowing that they did something as well as they possibly could, even though it took longer than it might have, or it wasn't done the easy way.

Isn't it interesting that we sometimes choose consciously to do something in a certain way that we know isn't the easiest way, because we feel that the harder way is the only "right" way to do it? Decisions like these are decisions about satisfaction. For example, I might choose to apologize to someone, saying face-to-face that I know I let him or her down, and I'm sorry my choice created that result. It would be easier for me to say that on the telephone; but I choose to speak those words personally, so that the other person knows this is important to me.

Maturity compels us to go beyond our comfort zones so that we can feel pride and respect for our own actions, rather than being satisfied with complacency, mediocrity, or disconnection from ideas and people and feelings that we value. A mature man can give up immediate pleasure for a higher cause. He can also give up personal pleasure to benefit other people, or to take an action that he simply knows is the "right" thing to do.

## Asking For Help

How hard is it for you to ask for help when you need it? You're going to need help.

Many men approach life with the attitude that they can do everything alone, and they don't need anyone's help. In their view, asking for help is a sign of weakness. For instance, I don't like reading manuals. When I buy something with written instructions, I often choose to ignore the manual (and possibly struggle) until I have done it alone, my own way. The manual is there to help me put it together; yet I lose patience and I don't want to read the details. I just want to get it done. We men have been taught to get things done, and we're fantastic at it. But the process of growing into manhood isn't the same as getting something done, and there isn't a manual that explains how to grow into manhood. Growth isn't a process of doing; it's a process of experiencing.

What will maturity feel like; how will I know I'm more mature than I used to be? The best answer I can give is to tell you that you'll recognize it when you begin to experience it, and it's a mystery until you've started to feel it. Mature masculinity is like the feeling of wind in your face. You know the wind is blowing but you can't see it. You can feel it on your skin, but you can't touch it or see it. You'll sense a shift inside you, a feeling, a knowing that you've started living differently. When you've felt this "knowing" inside of you, you'll gain confirmation from others that something has changed, in the way people speak to you. You might realize that you've stopped having the feeling that you'd rather "hide" than let people know what you're thinking or feeling.

Some men do live with a small piece of fear or shame (or a feeling that they're not important to anybody), that holds them back from "showing up" as the authentic man that they are. Without revealing the whole man, it's impossible to create the "full" relationships that we crave. If you've been a man who has "hidden," or has withdrawn from others instead of taking steps to have the closer relationship with them that you want, then you will definitely know when this has changed for you. When you are "present" (really "sensing what you're feeling inside") you will know the feeling of "intimacy," even though this intimacy is with yourself.

As you connect with your feelings in this way, you can begin to connect with others at the deepest levels. When you share what you know about yourself, you open the door to having true emotional intimacy with the people who matter most in your life.

This is the basis of intimate, loving relationships. Without intimacy, you're not experiencing the relationship you can create with another human being. It's only at this level of intimacy that our emotional needs as human beings can be met.

Knowing what you're feeling is the key that opens the universe inside you, and makes you available for deep connection. When someone is in this zone, they begin to recognize the feelings they've had: "I didn't get as angry as I used to, I said I'm sorry for the first time, I had more patience and became more understanding, I smiled, I did what I was afraid to do, I asked for what I needed, I felt sadness and joy, I cried today." These are statements that men speak when they are in this process. This is the process of emotional growth and maturity.

We all have emotions all our lives. The mature man can have those emotions, and honor them for what they are, and make decisions in his life that aren't the result of his fear or sadness or anger or shame. He can also ask for help without feeling weakness or shame, because he doesn't feel that having an emotion means that he lacks something. If a man needed a hammer to "do" something, he'd go buy a hammer without feeling diminished or ashamed. A mature man knows that he's responsible for getting what he needs emotionally. He can recognize his emotions and name them, and do the work of making assertive choices that don't harm him or others.

## I've asked for Help

Grown men do experience conflict of all sorts, and they realize that the best way to resolve a conflict is to ask for help. In the process of writing this book, I've felt conflict of my own. I realized that I want the book to be finished, and I've also realized that there is more and more that I want you to know, so I've experienced frustration about wanting to stop, and wanting to keep adding to the book.

I recently met a man that I immediately recognized as wise. I chose to trust my evaluation of his wisdom and his willingness to share his insights, and I brought this conflict to him with a request for help. I could have chosen to keep grinding away, with the same frustrating outcome. My sense of urgency came from inside of me, and parts of my emotional self were feeling frustration (fear and shame, actually), and especially fear that the book might never be done. It was time for a new way of seeing things, and I believed that this man would see my situation in a way that I wasn't seeing it.

My anxiety was a good thing; my body was telling me that I was feeling too much conflict, and that it was time to address that feeling. I was right about the man I asked for help, and the response I received was both affirming and constructive. He helped me to see myself in a new way, and to see that my frustration was a gift to me at this time. It was a true indication that I have a lot of feelings about this book. The book has a life of its own already, like a living child. The book has been a process, and it still is, and it's just as much a mystery as other growth experiences.

I needed to hear from someone I trusted that this experience of making a book is somewhat out of my control. I started it, and it keeps growing. Until I heard the response of the man I asked for help, I struggled to trust that it will be whatever it's supposed to be. He spoke words to me that I hadn't spoken to myself, and I needed to hear them. Inside I knew his words were the truth, and I could feel in my body that they were the truth. Now I can experience the process of creating the book as an act of creation, and it requires my trust and an ability to let go of expectations. This is possible for me because I know myself as a man of faith and trust.

The process of reaching manhood is not about getting to a particular place, completing a task, or achieving a goal. It is about being still and listening to the inner voice and paying close attention to what the truth feels like inside. Men who have reached maturity are witnesses to their own deepest experiences, and they know that they don't have a choice about what they feel or why they feel it. They accept their feelings as the most precious part of them. They trust and acknowledge the "truth" of their feelings, as guidance for the way they will choose to live. Their emotions are never an excuse for the choice of actions that they'll take. They make a choice about how to behave, even though they may be having powerful emotions, based on principles of behavior in their lives. It's what a man chooses to do with his emotions that empowers the man.

Boys are still told to lie about what they feel and what they think. Anger is the only emotion that so many men will encourage in their sons. "Softer" feelings signaling distress, pain, sadness, longing, hurt, and rejection are discouraged by the parents who want their sons to live without knowing the full repertoire of their experiences. They are willing to see their sons live with the same suffering that they have experienced in their own lives as parents.

These parents can't see that they're afraid for their sons, and they speak their experiences in words like these: "it's a tough world out there." They fear that having such emotional experiences will bring a disapproving reaction from others, possibly just a general fear that others will consider their sons to be "less manly" than other men. Parents who teach their children to deny the experience of fear are incapable of teaching their sons how to make good decisions that aren't controlled by fear. They can't teach that, because they haven't experienced it.

## Taking the Path of Manhood-- Conscious Desire

Steps along the way occur in this order: 1. Unconscious experiences of a desire to be more "knowledgeable" and more mature in the world. 2. Learning to recognize and become familiar with feelings, instead of denying them. 3. The conscious desire to identify and experience feelings, so that I can honor them for what they are, and make the "good" decisions that I need to make in my life, separate from the influence of fear or shame or anger or sadness (or even joy). The conscious desire to experience feelings is the mark of a man entering maturity.

The growth process begins with a young person who lacks the "consciousness" of his (or her) feelings; he has no familiarity with feelings. A young person describes his experience with words like "confusion" or "turmoil" or "wanting something that I can't identify." As the young man gains experience in identifying his feelings, he can begin to recognize what he could only identify as "confusion" at an earlier time, and then learn to "slow down" some of the experience, in order to become more familiar with it. This is one of the ways in which mature men describe what they experienced as their "desire to grow" has changed. It changed from being unconscious to becoming conscious.

This is also one of the experiences that is missing in the lives of parents who can't teach their sons to experience fear, for example. I want to see more parents in the world (and sons and daughters) who can honestly say this: "I recognize this feeling as fear from experience, and I can make choices that aren't determined by my fear." This is mature consciousness. Mature people can make good decisions in their lives that are not controlled (or influenced excessively) by the fact that they are experiencing strong feelings of sadness or fear or anger or shame or joy.

This growth experience often begins when boys begin to feel the influence of peer pressure, sometimes responding to it even more than the approval of their parents. The influence of peer pressure is another manifestation of the desire for approval. Again, we can see three steps along the way: 1. The child is born and is totally dependent on his parents for everything, and he has an irresistible need for the approval of his parents. 2. The older child begins to develop the first tentative sense of independence, in that he (or she) craves the approval of other grownups (as well as his own parents), and also craves the approval of his peers. 3. The mature person cares only that he approves of his own actions, and can disregard the responses of others, because he will only be satisfied with his life if the gifts he leaves behind are accomplishments he can look to with pride in himself; nothing else matters.

Notice that at a time of incomplete maturity, peer pressure can influence the boy much more than the approval of parents and other adults. The boy's need for peer approval is rarely acknowledged as an emotional "fact" by a boy; it's almost always denied, out of fear that showing a feeling will lead to being ostracized by his peers. So, he represses and denies what he is feeling and stuffs his pain deep inside. Notice, too, that it's also possible for a man to live his entire grown life stuck in this second phase of maturity, with a bigger desire for the approval of others than for his own approval. This is a consequence of refusing to experience feelings, to become familiar with them, and to learn to make "good" decisions, based on his own internal sense of conduct that is worthy of respect.

No one can force a man to grow into authentic masculinity; it's a set of choices that each man has to make. We may feel threatened by someone such as a loved one, or fear losing a job because our behavior has gotten to the point where others around you are having difficulties coping with our actions. We can seek help that is prompted by others and go through the motions of healing, but not heal. I cannot stress enough that unless we choose a healing path, we'll remain childlike, and we won't grow emotionally into feeling like grown men. There must come a time when we can no longer settle for the way that WE feel about ourselves.

At that time, we can accept that the way we're behaving is no longer serving us and the others in our lives. The boyish attitude, the denial of emotion, the lack of truth we speak, the lies we tell ourselves and others, and the way we act, will all fail to satisfy us for another day. When we've had the conscious moment of refusing to be satisfied with the life we've created for ourselves (so far), we can make the conscious choice to want more than anything to find a new way of living that will be a source of joy and satisfaction, both for ourselves and for the people we care about.

## You are not an Island: Conscious Healing

Once you have consciously made a choice to integrate the parts of yourself that have remained hidden, the next step is to take action. There are many tools for healing yourself. I'll discuss the basics and let you begin exploring from here.

No matter where you choose to begin, know that you're not on this path alone. Actually, you'll need to admit and accept that growing up is done with the help of others. You will no longer be functioning as though you're the center of the universe, but you are part of a larger system.

You may already be a man who has begun reading the words of others in a conscious search for greater understanding of his feelings, and of his way of functioning in the world. If you are, then you already know that others have taken the time to offer you a piece of the puzzle, and you can find the information that is waiting for you. Reading the words of others will help broaden your understanding of the processes of self-healing, helping you to lay a cognitive foundation that will help you recognize when you are "on" your healing path, and when your efforts are not moving you forward.

Some men struggle most of their lives with the need to achieve perfection in everything they do. This work of growing into a man isn't about achieving perfection. It's about staying fully aware of what is real in your life, and the choices you will make, and whether those choices will bring results into your life that serve you or cause you harm of some kind. Your feelings are real, and with experience you'll feel them in your body. When you feel them inside, you won't choose to minimize them or disregard them, because you'll trust them like the advice of a loving father. You'll be continuously aware of those feelings, because the feelings will tell you whether your choices are bringing joy and satisfaction into your life. In this new, conscious awareness of the information your feelings bring you, you'll know whether your choices are bringing you the results that you value in your life, or whether new choices are necessary.

Once you've chosen to heal yourself, and have felt the benefits of the first small successes, you'll see the *Big Choice* that you face. Will you return to the older ways of being "boyish," refusing to accept responsibility for whether you are happy in life? My hope for you is that you will not be able to short-change yourself any longer. My hope is that you'll see the harm you bring into your life by making choices that are not based on the information your feelings bring you about whether your choices are good ones or bad.

Your ability to recognize your feelings in your body is the basis of making good choices in your life. "What do you feel in your gut about this or that?" "What is your truth about what you've got to do next, what's true for you?" When you recognize the ways in which your body brings you the answers to questions through feelings, you will know that your life has already changed and the old ways will never be good enough again.

With the old ways, you would feel less respect for yourself. You'd feel uncomfortable knowing you are not living in your "truth," because you know there's something you need to do for yourself, and you aren't doing it. Once you know how to feel your "truth," the only choices you'll be proud of are choices that move you forward on your growth path. It will be possible for you to deny your truth, and to regress toward the old ways (whatever they were). But you will have experienced the power of your own choices as the key to your happiness, and that experience will never go away.

## What you don't know can kill you—
## Factors to Consider

When a man chooses a healing way, instead of living by lies, he remains a boy inside. The path may be unpredictable. For example, if you take a trip on a vacation, you know where you may be going, but as you are driving you suddenly get a flat tire, or get sick from something you ate, or the weather becomes so bad that you have to change your plans. In other words, the details of the path are difficult to know. No one has complete access to all the knowledge required for our journeys. All you know is that you have a destination. The process may take you to places you have not been before. You learn new information about yourself you knew nothing about.

In starting out, each man also needs the help of a medical or psychiatric doctor in establishing that unknown physical problems are the cause of an emotional struggle, hiding a man's authenticity. Many medical or psychiatric problems can be the cause of emotional problems; and the emotional problems that result can't be dealt with effectively until the unknown causes have also been treated effectively. Many people suffer from depression because their bodies can't produce the right amounts of chemicals that are required for humans to experience happiness. There are also psychiatric disturbances that can remain undetected for many years, including ADHD (attention deficit hyperactivity disorder) and bipolar disorder, among many others. Any unknown problem will be a barrier in a man's growth process.

I'll give you an example. A man who has been using alcohol or drugs for 15 years decides to stop using. In this process of recovery, he begins accepting that he is medicating his long-standing depression with alcohol, which started in his early teens. As long as he uses chemicals, he masks his depression. Now that he is free from chemicals, he is feeling more depressed. In his healing process, he may need an antidepressant to chemically stabilize himself. With proper medication his depression is reduced as he continues in recovery. Prior to sobriety, he did not know he had a long-standing depression. As a sober man, he can accept the limitations of his body chemistry and know what his body needs.

When a man takes ownership of his life, he pays attention to what he needs, and being accountable, he meets his needs in healthy ways. What he once disregarded as trivial and unimportant, he can now appreciate differently, for how he relates with others and what others have to say. He is multi faceted and multi-dimensional rather than having one dimension. In the one dimensional state of being, not all the pieces are available. He is unable to see the forest for the trees. This is the false sense of being in the world, not taking into account other variables that play into his life. He can now see more because he is more.

There is a very direct relationship between our bodies and our emotional well-being. The bodily functions act as one unit. If there are unhealthy biological functions requiring medical interventions, our emotional and psychological functions are also not balanced. The same is true if our psychological and emotional makeup is in denial. Denial of our truth leads to sickness in the body. Emotions must be expressed in one form or another. The truth must be told. The more conscious one becomes, the more we are able to detect what is going on in our bodies, our minds, our feelings.

## Meetings the Needs of the Boy

Sometimes we say that the "the Boy" is still present in "the Man," and we usually say that with respect and compassion. If the boy is hungry he must be fed. If the boy is tired, he must rest and sleep. If the boy is sad and lonely, he must cry. If the boy was emotionally betrayed, he must fully share his story in a safe place. If the boy was deprived of physical contact, he must be touched by others. If the boy felt unwanted and unloved, he must be loved and validated. These needs that we think of as the needs of the boy are also present in the man. There are no shortcuts to meeting the boy's needs. The needs must be met, and the boy needs help in meeting them; he simply can't do it for himself. The mature man accepts that these needs are part of being a living human being, and he chooses to have relationships in his life, as one of the greatest possible sources of joy. This is where our needs are met, both for the boy and for the man.

## Freeing the Child to Become a Man

If we are to heal as men we need to do the job from within the self where it all originated. Half measures will not fix man's wounds. Pacifying him with more stuff to divert his attention from the self will only bring him more dead-end emptiness.

Developing mature masculinity has already begun because today's men have started to awaken from the traditional restrictive role expectations that have given way somewhat in this culture to more heterogeneous role expectations for both men and women. Freed from these restrictive expectations, men are beginning to realize that their lives have been governed by fear rather than love.

A man who lives his life judging whether his feelings are "okay," based on expectations, is experiencing only fear (or shame) as the driving force in his life. Fear drives are naturally developed when a man cannot fully express his unique emotional self in the here and now. Men hide their emotions from others, including other men. Men collude with each other in a silent conspiracy whose unconscious aim is to suppress emotional truth. Yet, a surge of electricity sparks a man into awakening when he hears another man speak his truth. It is as though the man has been blinded for years, and can finally begin to see. It's my premise that too many men haven't heard emotional truth from their fathers, and the longing for an emotionally truthful father is just waiting in a peripheral aspect of the self.

Men's lives are violent because their souls have been violated. The old world paradigm can no longer sustain the needs of our civilization. Cooperation, negotiation, and working for mutually beneficial goals are the only ways to continue to thrive in the rapidly evolving industrialized world. It is up to each of us individually to choose transformation from the warrior-like persona that our civilization promotes, to change into a more loving, mission-driven inner warrior whose satisfaction is not based on conquering, power, and glory, but on building and sustaining emotionally healthy systems where no one loses and everyone benefits.

Wars, domestic violence between partners, and gang affiliations are some of the extreme conditions in which men "live out" their fear. The false idea is that a man must maintain control if he is going to get his needs met. We men often control through intimidation, violence, and oppression. The distortion here is that there is not enough power and control to go around, not enough to satisfy all men. One or more of us must be denied, and each of us needs to do whatever is in his power to prevent others from getting what they want. The premise is that a man will be less or get less if another man gets something. The notion that all of our needs can be met seems like an insane idea, because it contradicts the model

121

of competition between us, for everything we value. We cannot co-exist in the same space. One of us must fail.

This is the old-world-order mentality. It worked for many centuries, but it has stopped working. It cannot sustain this world as it did, because more and more systems interact at the same time, and one person is incapable of controlling (or influencing) all of them. Each of us must learn to cooperate, to get what we need. Our needs can exist and be met at the same time.

We have pushed the envelope and our civilization demands that we cooperate. Without cooperation, it only those who have chosen to take the higher ground and look within who will outlive the "old order." The rest of us will die off through the process of "natural selection." Wars, sickness and stress will kill off the ones who can't adapt. The new way responds like a willow tree. No matter how strong the wind blows, the branches have the flexibility to bend with the wind and not attempt to control the wind by resisting. The branch that has no flexibility will crack and fall off the tree, and so will the old-world order of men.

The new world order incorporates a man whose spirituality is open. He takes into account everything. He is not dogmatic to any particular point of view. He can listen and understand differences and empower others by giving to them rather than taking from them. He may follow a religious practice and rituals, but he is grounded in the spirituality that he feels inside his body, and not from his intellect.

In these moments a man is connected to his humanity. He understands that his spirituality comes from his divinity, which he got by being born. He is loved because he is human. His birth is a gift, and his development is to accept his life fully. He develops an appreciation that he is just a part of a larger system. He is in the universe and contains all the particles that are in the cosmos, but he is not the center. This realization drives everything he does; and his behavior is mission-driven, knowing he serves himself by serving the ones he cares about. He can find a source of divinity within himself; he finds his archetypal king by serving his family and his community. He has an understanding of what gets in the way of connecting with others, rather than justifying his conduct and making others adjust to his wants and needs. He embraces life. He knows he is not perfect and realizes he will never achieve perfection. He strives to regulate his needs with the needs of others and accepts accountability for his behavior rather than blaming others for his shortcomings.

The process that each man must experience is the process that he was told not to attempt. In order for a man to heal, he must disengage from all the rubbish and lies he was told to believe. The process he was taught, which is actually inhumane, was how he became "civilized." He has forgotten his human side that continues to hunger to live in the world as the natural man he really can become. As a man gains maturity, he distills his experiences as patterns that have succeeded in bringing satisfaction to his life. I call these guiding principles. You may call them something else in your own life.

## Guiding Principles

The result of making good choices in my life is that I can rely upon my awareness of the patterns in my good choices. Awareness is the integration of emotions and thoughts. When I have a hard decision to make, or I'm struggling to know what's right for me to do, I can trust the awareness that I've gained as a good indication of what my "right" choice will be. I've learned that the right choices that I've made are always choices that strengthen my relationships with others and affirm my sense of the man that I am. My path has been a path of gaining love and acceptance for that man, and that continues to be my path. As I engage in my life, I'm aware of these guiding principles below.

1.  We humans all come from the same life force. We are sacred beings in human bodies. Our authentic selves are expressions of our divine inheritance. All that is life-affirming in each of us is a reflection of our divine nature.

2.  Each of us is empowered to create all of the joy in our lives that we desire, and it is up to us to find it and fulfill it on earth. Our awareness, which includes all our senses, is a vehicle to guide us toward that joy.

3.  Understanding and recognizing our emotions is vital for discovering our authentic selves. To deny the emotional experiences that each of us has is to deny ourselves the gift of our humanity. Thoughts and feelings are expressions of our humanity.

4. Our feelings are expressions of our spirit and soul. If you stop eating, you will get sick and die. We do not choose our feelings. They function to keep us aware so that we get what we need, to grow into maturity.

5. All experiences, positive and negative, are there to help us mature into fully conscious, loving and generous beings.

6. What I deny as truth will be revealed in unhealthy patterns and expressions in the way I think and the way I act. The universe has no room for secrets. It all comes out one way or another towards the light.

7. I am not ultimately in charge of my life. There are higher forces at work at any one time that are beyond my comprehension and independent of my will. I trust that I am where I need to be in my journey.

8. I live my life in gratitude and compassion, because of the gifts in my life that I can now recognize, as I guide my life by principle.

I've relied on the principles above in my life, as the awareness that guides my choices. As your awareness grows, you'll be recognizing the patterns among your own right choices that have strengthened your relationships and affirmed your sense of the man you are. It is my wish that this process will strengthen and guide you on your path of growth.

Remember that even a mature man can become confused, and then disconnect, and lose consciousness of how his behavior might affect another person. Men who act without awareness of the results of their behavior harm themselves, especially when they have relationships with the people they are harming. Ultimately every man is responsible for the consequences of his actions. All he can do when his life goes out of control is feel remorse for the damage he has created around him. This is the starting point for his journey back to the man he can become.

# Chapter 9
# Curiosity Can Heal You

You have gotten this far reading this book. That should tell you something about yourself. It should tell you that you have a curiosity, you are seeking, and you are searching for something different to happen in your life. You may be hungry to feel different about yourself. You may even know something is not right inside you. It all starts with you. Whatever it may be, it needs attention. There is a sense of urgency and it cannot be put on hold any longer. This is a good sign. It means that your body can no longer contain the discomfort. It's like a boiling teakettle. As the water boils, the pressure must be released somewhere.

You may feel this same pressure. It must be let out now. You may even know you need something, but you're not sure what. Perhaps this is the first book you ever read about something related to you. What is important is that you have made a choice. You've chosen for yourself to do something different. What is important is that you know something needs fixing. It's time for some emotional house cleaning.

There are basically two kinds of guys. One kind is content with "just getting by" emotionally. Feelings are uncomfortable and unwelcome burdens. "I'd rather be numb than sad; I'd rather be angry than hurt; I'd rather be isolated than needy." They never look back, "taking stock" of their lives. I'm sure you don't know anybody like that. The other kind of guy won't settle for anything less than joy in his life. He knows that feelings are the most reliable indicators of what he values in his life. He knows that men who are just surviving are actually choosing to live their lives, filled with unexpressed or denied pain. He chooses to thrive emotionally. He also wants to make the world a better place, because he lived here. Which kind of guy are you? Which kind of guy do you want to be?

## Where and How to Start-- Learning the Signals of Your Body

You need to know that you have already started. By reading a book like this, you have begun the journey. It isn't the feeling of having a knot in your gut, or sweaty palms, or the urge to scream. It's that you've made a choice. It isn't so important the types of healing paths you take as much as being conscious that you have decided to start healing.

What needs to heal? We all start this process wherever the struggle leads us to start. It may be in your work relationships, your family of origin, your marriage, your children, a major loss, or just the feeling that you're not the man you've always wanted to be. These are points of entry into the healing path.

As you explore yourself more, these entry points will eventually become less important. The issues will shift as you shift. Eventually as you continue in your path, a deeper understanding of core themes will emerge, identifying the needs that are not met.

As you activate this awareness of the ways in which your needs aren't being met, you will come to know these needs and respect them. You will respect these needs in ways that you have not respected and honored them as a young man. How will you recognize these needs? The simple answer is that you'll start listening to the signs you can recognize, telling you that you're experiencing emotions as feelings within your body. A feeling of tightness in your chest might "match up" with anger or fear or sadness in you. Only you can recognize these signs that identify your feelings.

When you experience one of these signs, give yourself a moment to identify and name the emotion you're feeling. What's going on in your life? Make that connection. It's part of the growth process, and part of your growing awareness of your emotions. Identifying that feeling, and tracing it back to its root in your experiences, is key to liberating yourself from that pattern in your life. Why am I angry so often? Why do I feel abandoned when someone I care about doesn't agree with me?

You aren't having these reactions for the first time today. This is almost certainly a pattern in your life. Once you recognize the pattern, you can break it, by making a conscious choice to accept that this pattern isn't serving you and the people you care about. You can choose to speak to yourself with words like these:

"I know I've felt abandoned before, but I don't have to feel abandoned in the same way today. I'm a grown man, and I'm not diminished or threatened by the fact that I disagree with someone I care about. We've disagreed before, and this person didn't leave me. I know we can get through this by acknowledging our disagreement. And I can create a new pattern by recognizing that the old pattern of my emotional behavior isn't working for me anymore. I can change."

Know the signals from within your body, like tightness in the stomach, shortness of breath, rapid speech, poor eye contact, heart palpations, rapid heart rate, twitching, and restlessness. These may all be signals that you are having emotions that you can recognize and deal with in new ways.

Each of us has his unique body signals. Recognizing these signals can lead to acknowledging our feelings. As we get to know ourselves more and more, some of these body signals may subside and turn into one particular signal, such as tightness in the stomach. For the most part, the solar plexus (the entire area surrounding your belly) is the most sensitive area where the body signals that there are feelings. Many of the clients I have worked with have found their abdomen to be the place where they can access their feelings, in the solar plexus. The abdomen is connected to breathing. Breathing fully allows free expression of feeling. Shallow breathing reflects repressed feelings; our stomachs then get tight and constricted, and we feel a struggle inside. When this happens, the key is to undo what we have learned and not ignore the feeling that is being activated. Just let it happen. Releasing it to the light, giving it the honor it deserves, the feeling is completed, the experience is full, the learning is complete.

Feelings teach us what our bodies know we need to do: to cry if we are going through a loss, to laugh if we're experiencing joy, to feel angry if we've been betrayed, and to feel sad if we've been hurt. Being in touch with the authentic truth of what we're experiencing keeps us grounded in the present, knowing what we are feeling, knowing what it is that we need to do. This is the training that is required, in order to begin integrating the immature man inside the mature man. That is how we begin to achieve full masculine maturity.

## Humans Experience Losses as Though They're Wounds

Our nature as humans guarantees that no matter what, each of us somehow will be "wounded." Each of us is imperfect, and each of us will also take actions that harm another person. An essential lesson is taught by each of the wounding experiences. The lesson is to know what it feels like to have an experience without joy, where there should be joy in the young child's life. Instead, there's just sadness over the loss of this joy, with no clear way of overcoming the loss. Often it remains an incomplete experience for years. It can't be more complete until the child (or young man) is mature enough to make the conscious choice to remember (and re-experience) how fully and deeply he felt the pain of that loss, so that he can "release" that incomplete part of the wounding experience, and create a situation in which he can actually experience some (or all) of the joy that he could have felt long ago, even if it now takes just the form of relief that a long period of suffering has ended.

The person who chooses to heal in this way can become the man he has dreamed about being. Bringing forth this man that he dreamed of becoming is solely the responsibility of each man, because it requires a conscious choice that can only be made by each man. Making that choice brings access to the joy that is inherently a part of a "whole" life experience. Through a man's choices he can live as a loving force in the world; and his life will have meaning and purpose. It is up to each man to seek and discover that meaning and purpose. This purpose is the answer to the question that many men ask at different times in their lives: "Why am I here?"

The man who asks "why am I here?" is standing on the line that separates the struggle for survival from the ability to thrive emotionally, living in joy. Until he experiences the terrible losses fully, he has no comprehension of the part that he hasn't permitted to happen, often because it was just too painful. The conscious choice to revisit that loss, and experience all of the emotions that come up, is the choice that brings meaning to a man's life.

For example, a man might feel so betrayed by the sweetheart he loved so dearly, that he chooses never to be so vulnerable to disappointment and pain and sadness again. By choosing to remember (and re-experience) the events of that betrayal, and all his terrible sadness, he might find affirmation of his strength after the betrayal, and affirmation that others find him attractive and desirable, and he might learn that the loneliness he still finds is because he has chosen to avoid intimacy with another because it leaves him vulnerable to pain. And he might learn that he could have found what he has always craved, if he was willing to risk another disappointment to gain everything he wanted.

In this brave moment, he can find the meaning of that experience in his life, if he sees and accepts that loving relationships only exist where trust and emotional vulnerability stand side by side. With that new understanding, he can choose to thrive, instead of just surviving.

Every time a man chooses to control or override his feelings in an emotionally painful experience, he chooses just to survive in his life, rather than take the risks that would permit him to thrive emotionally, in order to live with joy and a full understanding of the meaning of his life.

## The Lessons of the Losses

If a man feels no emotions, it's almost always because he has chosen to stop feeling them. If he has chosen to stop feeling them, he can never learn what those feelings can teach him. Was there a moment in your life when something happened that felt so terrible, that you chose to protect yourself "for the rest of your life?" Maybe you even spoke words like these: "I'll never let that happen to me again, and I hope to live long enough that I can't even remember it."

The man who makes a choice like that thinks that he'll stop feeling sad and lonely and depressed and unmotivated if he turns off his feelings. Instead, he simply loses the ability to identify the emotions he's experiencing. And when he loses the ability to identify those feelings, he doesn't just lose the ability to learn about himself. He also loses the ability to connect with others in the deep and meaningful ways that all humans need, and that characterize us as human beings. What a terrible loss it would be, always to feel (and be) alone, because of the fear of feeling pain again. What a terrible choice to make.

That's why we choose to go back to the clear memories of our losses, intentionally, to a time just before we made the choice to turn off the feelings and forget the memories. We do this so that we can actually remember how truly sad, or hopeless, or powerless,

133

or unworthy of love we may have felt in a time of overwhelming loss.

When we are willing to remember that loss clearly, our bodies begin again to give us the clues about what we were feeling. In a way, it's amazing to me that the "feelings" can almost always be felt again; and all we have to do is turn them back on again, by giving ourselves permission to take the risk of experiencing feelings again. We return to the moment when we were feeling terrible, and we feel it again, so that we can recognize the feelings again, and let them happen.

Why would anybody choose to feel that way again? Because they finally realize that they're failing to have close connections with people they care about, because they don't even understand what their loved ones are feeling. They begin to realize that the only way to bring value and happiness into their lives is through connection with others. When they're ready to re-join the human race, the only choice they can make is to take the risk of feeling pain again. They go back to the memory of a terrible feeling, so that they can experience it, and begin to feel the kind of "release" that a person feels when a huge emotion builds up, and then reaches a peak, and then begins to fade away. The pain actually does begin to fade away, and this is an important lesson.

As a child, you were powerless, and your experiences may have left a lasting impact. For example, if you had a father who was an alcoholic and emotionally abused you, what happened was clearly beyond your control. The abuse you experienced is a part of your personal history; it's a fact, a piece of data about your life. Your experience at such a time would probably be emotionally painful; and you may also have felt physical pain. Your interpretation of this experience, as a child, was that you felt unloved. Like many other people in such a situation, you may also have felt unworthy of love; and you may even have felt that you did something terrible to make yourself unworthy of being loved, because the situation was overwhelming and incomprehensible. The impacts of these early experiences can last into adulthood.

To begin the process of healing, you must first acknowledge the "objective" pieces of the loss you felt, so that the loss seems just like a set of facts being provided intellectually by your memory. Then, as your awareness and recognition deepen, you can begin to acknowledge the emotional experience. The emotional pain we experience is reflection of a terrible struggle inside. You might think that the pain is a reflection of how hard it is to release the emotion connected to a loss; and this usually isn't true. Much more frequently the pain is what we experience as we resist against releasing the pain, and as we resist the emotional release. This moment of release is an opportunity to give yourself the honor or the worthiness to be loved that was not given to you in that experience of loss.

Often, this first experience of emotional release brings us to an experience of our bodies, in a moment of internal rest, or internal peace. What I viewed as a painful experience is transformed into a gift, and it's for me. I've given myself something that was withheld. Imagine, or remember, how powerful and liberating a moment like that can be. As you honor the emotion you've carried for a long time, you can experience it again as a more complete experience of a more complete human being. This inner witnessing of the more complete person can be recognized as connection with feeling, and it could be labeled as inward love. With increased experience, this "love of self" extends to others. You once felt like an unloved and unworthy being, and you transform yourself into a loving (and loved) and worthy being. As a loving being you can now be of service to others. As a man, as a father, as a partner, you stand as a whole person.

Our human nature is to protect ourselves from anything that we perceive as a threat. From our earliest emotional wounding experiences, we begin to create a view of how the world works and how relationships work. Early childhood experiences are the building blocks for how we go about living our adult lives. We set up and create our adult relationships based on the earlier imprints of how we have perceived others and ourselves. What is key here is that unless an adult figure provided the space for us to have a full emotional response, the emotional "charge" of young experiences can stay within us. On the other hand, a child who had the space in which to express himself fully can learn how to deal with the discomfort of his feelings. This discomfort is a real experience of the body. The natural response is to want to stop feeling the discomfort, and to ask questions that will bring him some relief.

I remember a clear example of this ability, when I had a mother and her son in my office. The father was not present in the home, due to an incident of domestic violence that led to police intervention. The boy's mother told the father to leave the house indefinitely, and got an order of protection. In our family sessions, the child began asking when his father would come back home. The boy was naturally curious and was asking very direct questions. At one point, his mother told him that she didn't know when his father would be returning home, and this led to further questions.

This mother was very loving and supportive. She was in tune with her son and had a sense of what he could and couldn't understand. At one point, she said she wasn't sure if he would come back at all, not giving him any false hope. In response, the son closed his eyes and puffed up his mouth, looking like he was holding his breath, and apparently not wanting to feel the meaning of what he had just heard. This was a natural response. He literally forced himself to pause briefly, and to experience and control what he was feeling. Even though the mother was providing a caring and loving environment, his natural response was to defend himself from his feelings in that moment.

He recognized the pain of that moment, and he didn't want to feel it. His mother let him experience it in his own way, and her restraint was a supportive response, in his opportunity for emotional growth. She demonstrated repeatedly that she was paying close attention to her son's responses, and she continued to examine and evaluate her responses to her son, during the course of our sessions together.

As this child grows up, he will almost certainly remember coming to counseling with his mother. It would be naïve to believe he'll feel no consequences from the absence of his father, just because his mother brought him to counseling. On the other hand, though, his mother was doing all she could to provide a holding environment for her son by communicating with her son, by allowing him to have his own feelings, by being honest and caring with him.

She respected the importance of allowing him to have his own experience by giving him as much information as he was capable of integrating at that time. Despite her own issues with her marriage, she was able to set herself aside and focus on her son's emotional needs.

It wasn't the mother's job to protect her son from the reality of his life. The reality was that his father was not home and he wanted his father to come back home. He had no control over these events. All he could do was to accept the reality of his life at that time. His mother's primary focus was not to give him any false hope and not to deny him the reality that perhaps his father would never return home. His mother's job was to allow the son to fully experience himself as he was, a hurt boy who longed for his father.

As harsh as it may sound, his mother acted natural and realistic. She ultimately believed that he would handle his pain and accept his life as it was given to him as long as she acted in loving ways towards him. That is all his mother was expected to do. She stepped up to the plate and acted effectively. In essence, she was empowering her son and coaching him to be authentic. In his own natural way of being, he was encouraged and not discouraged from experiencing his feelings and dealing with them as they come up.

## There are No Accidents, Only Experiences

We are spiritual beings having a human experience. Reality is much more mysterious than what we can perceive with our five senses. Every living thing is made up of the same molecular structures. As I mentioned earlier, the universe leaves nothing by chance. Every living thing has its own life force with a particular purpose for its creation. Everything living serves a function and a purpose. When it comes to human beings, our task is to discover our purpose and ultimate mission for our existence. Everything that we experience is to serve this goal.

How can our creator create chaos, pain, destruction, and accidents in the human experience? It's in our very nature as humans that our wounding experiences motivate us to serve a higher purpose. They give meaning to our efforts to relieve suffering in the world. Without wounds, we would have no sense of mission. Each man's mission might be to heal the wound he has experienced, in all the other people in the world who've felt the same wound.

If you come to accept that we co-create our lives, then you embrace the part of your life that has caused you pain. Co-creating means that you have a partnership in how life unfolds. You have no control over some of what you experience. Co-creating is developing an attitude that no matter what has happened in your life it is for an ultimate good for you and for others. It is not so much our task to judge what is good for us. What is our task is to do our very best with what we have. The richness in our lives is inherited by the accumulation of our wisdom and experience. I have met wealthy individuals who were bankrupt when it came to self-love and being loved by others; and I have met with those who had little but they felt rich inside. It is not the accumulation of things that makes us full, but the fulfillment we can feel in our daily experiences.

I think of the actor Christopher Reeve that was known to play Superman. Yes, he had an accident that was beyond his control. From this accident, he created new meaning in his life. His meaning stems from how he chose to deal with his accident. He did not crumple into oblivion, nor was he victimized by his misfortune. Instead, he chose to live with dignity and bring forth a greater purpose from his accident. Imagine how much more powerful this man has become by his example, compared to the role he played as Superman. Who was the real superman, the man before or after his accident? He demonstrated a higher level of existence in which he modeled for others how to live with what we have. There are many people who have taken adversity and turned it into something greater. Causes are created, movements are developed, challenges are conquered, inventions are discovered, poems and great books are written. The seed of our greatest potential may have started with a thorn and snapshot moments of darkness. Christopher Reeve has left a huge gift for all of us, in his response to the experiences of his life.

## Boy's Passion for Living

Take yourself to a time, a moment in which you felt uplifted, whether it was when you were a child, playing as many children play for hours totally immersed in their play, or when you were captivated by the beauty of a sunset, a piece of music, an event, a piece of writing, a scent, the feeling of a new love. This is the passion that runs in being human. We were meant to have passion, to feel it, and to live life as though this is the only day we have left. Breathing fully in the moment, savoring all of it, is a feast of your favorite foods just for you. The passion needs to flow to feel alive, just like our blood running through our veins, to be present in our life, to stay connected to the real.

Passion is experienced to the degree that we allow ourselves to feel the spectrum of our emotional lives. Attempts to control the flow of our emotions will lessen the degree of passion we have in our life. Some of us have more passion than others. This is due to the degree we allow ourselves to experience all there is for us to experience. Even though each one of us has a unique and personal path, collectively it leads to the same source, which is our human ability to experience joy.

## Living as a Man with the Boy Inside

Acting like a man and being a man is separating the men from the boys. When a man is in his authenticity, he no longer pretends to be anything other than himself. He can decipher what is inside himself and choose how to respond. He knows the difference between wearing a mask and being fully present.

A man becomes a man when he finally accepts that within himself he is also a boy. He gets to know this boy in every way. He knows what has caused him pain, what made him cry, what made him laugh. He discovers what this boy needs and knows how to take care of him. He knows when this boy is afraid or hurt and asks for help. He allows this boy to experience fully the life he lives as man. He has become comfortable inside his own skin. He finally understands that the boy inside needs love and deserves to be loved by others. He finally allows himself to give love and receive it freely from others. He is no longer chained by misconceptions or living in "shoulds". He is his own authority by staying authentic inside.

It takes courage to live in authenticity, to listen to yourself and not betray the boy inside you. Think of the "neediness" in you as being the boy. He's a very real part of the grown man that you are. You have a sacred contract with him, a bond and a promise, to keep him safe, to protect him not by isolating him or shutting him down or even making others wrong and you right, but by teaching him to know what his truth is and to speak his truth even when he is afraid. He knows he can rely on you to get him what he needs. You allow him to play in safe ways, and take him to places where he will feel nourished inside. You teach him about what it means to live with self-reliance and in relationship with others. You allow him to be alone when he needs to be by himself to regroup, but he knows he does not have to live alone any more.

Once again the boy is allowed to have dreams, knowing he can trust that you will help live his dreams. The more you take care of him the more he will trust you. His trust will be based on your commitment to him. The more he senses you are his ally the more he will relax and know you are always there. In essence, he will come to depend on you and his life is dependent on you.

You're the surgeon that can heal his wound. This is the challenge. You're the man that can take care of the part of you that recognizes your needs.

As men grow in this way, many find a deepening of compassion and gratitude in their lives. Many find a deepening and strengthening of their spiritual nature. Such a man understands that he is in a life process that is ever changing, always moving, and a part of the entire universe. He understands that he is mortal and has a limited time on earth, and therefore, he has an appreciation for what he does with his time. He values his life and the lives of

142

others. As a mortal man, he has discovered that he is not perfect and perfection cannot be achieved. Yet, his idea of perfection is not based on being flawless. His idea of perfection is that all of him was divinely created. He might feel that his body and mind were formed in God's image. He might find faith that there is a God who has brought life into consciousness. Regardless of the source of creation that he finds, he knows that he is a manifestation, a life force, in which sparks of light can be created by being fully human.

## Living with Connection

There's sad truth in the words of the comedian George Carlin, who once said: "The paradox of our time in history is that we have taller buildings, but shorter tempers, wider freeways, but narrower viewpoints. We spend more, but have less, we buy more, but enjoy less. We have bigger houses and smaller families, more conveniences, but less time. We have more degrees but less sense, more knowledge, but less judgment, more experts, yet more problems, more medicine but less wellness. We learned how to make a living, but not a life. We've added years to life not life to years. We've been all the way to the moon and back, but we have trouble crossing the street to meet a new neighbor. We conquered outer space but not inner space. We've cleaned up the air, but polluted the soul. We've conquered the atom, but not our prejudice. We write more, but learn less. We plan more, but accomplish less. These are the times of fast foods and slow digestion, big men and small character, steep profits and shallow relationships. These are the days of two incomes but more divorces, fancier houses, but broken homes."

To capture the real and not miss the essentials in life, we must stop and ask the question that has been asked by our great sages throughout the ages. Who are we and why are we here? What is our purpose and how can we fulfill it?

I've finally grown up now. The part of me that is the boy is alive, and he feels things he never felt before the man was grown. He appreciates the snapshot moments, the faces that he sees on a daily basis. In a much deeper way the boy values what he has needed all along; and now he's getting it. He values the love that each day brings. With each sunset, he is comforted by the stillness of the night in which he can finally say, "I've come home. Now I'm connected to the people I care about. I love my life, and I'm grateful for each day. I live out my life with intention. I can look back on my life with satisfaction."

# Chapter 10
# Shame is a Killer

Shame is one of the heaviest burdens a man can carry. For many men, it's almost impossible to put this burden down and walk away. Men who haven't experienced shame may find it difficult to connect with the suffering and the pain of men in shame. I invite those men to have compassion for the men in shame as they read this piece, and to have gratitude that they've lived with more joy in their lives than shame allows.

## Beginning to Know Shame

Shame is so complex that it nearly defies intellectual understanding. If you've ever participated in a conversation about shame, you've probably noticed how attractive it seems to be to engage in speculation about what causes shame, rather than focusing on the impacts of shame and the ways to get out from under its crushing weight. In one man's life, shame may take the form of a "tape recording" always playing in his head, bringing him the message that he's wrong about everything, or he's weak or unattractive, or maybe he'll never amount to anything, or his life is meaningless. In another man's life it may be a nearly frantic need for more "affirmation" of his value to others than he can ever hope to receive. We can describe symptoms like "hopelessness" and "lack of self-worth" over and over without gaining insight into the experience of the ones who are struggling with it.

What are they actually experiencing? Shame removes all meaning from a person's "existence" as though he or she has no "right to exist." Shame is an existence question. It's an existence question because when a person experiences shame, he takes actions (or refuses to act) in ways that remove all possibility of joy and satisfaction from his life. When that happens, there's nothing left but anger and fear and sadness and shame, and that's not a human emotion set. That leaves out more than half of what makes us human (by leaving out joy), and what's left isn't enough.

As humans, we're driven to experience joy and satisfaction; humans are all about the experience of joy. That's why it's an existence question, and that's why these men are fighting for their lives. This is one of the hardest demons to kill or acknowledge, because it's an active energy that challenges the human's right to exist, and works hard to keep him from feeling that he is alive; it's an energy that shuts down human emotional response. Shame challenges our right to exist.

Part of the impulse of shame is to kill off the parts that don't fit the model of shame, possibly expressed in words like "you'll never be good enough; won't you ever learn that simple fact about yourself?" A person might also feel that every time he experiences optimism or hope, he's disappointed again, and each time the disappointment is more bitter, until he shuts down the impulse to have trusting or loving relationships (so why keep trying?), or goes from job to job because it seems impossible to satisfy supervisors (again, why keep trying?) That's the active energy component of shame. Shame can be so thoroughly disguised that men use their accomplishments (wealth or academic credentials, or fame) to "balm their shame," without addressing the underlying problem.  Even the way a person lives simply isn't good enough.  No matter what the subject matter, "it" is never enough; and we humans will go to addiction and other forms of substitutes for joy, always looking for the lasting pleasure that can't be found.

Shame whispers "I'm not worthy to live."  It's about living and dying.  Shame is always there to tell a man that his life has no value—he's already dead, and nothing will bring him back to life.  Shame has a face.  Shame is a killer.

## Overcoming Denial

Overcoming the denial is the first step in moving out from under the shadow of shame.

Shame lives in the mind, where it kills off all possibility of the human emotion of joy.  When joy is dead, shame moves on to kill off all the remaining emotions, to complete the murder of the soul.  In some ways it disguises itself, convincing the person in shame that "this is the way grownups see the world."

Shame works so effectively that a person will often deny the existence of the shame that he (or she) is feeling.  Why would that be true?  It's because they're ashamed to be ashamed.  As long as that denial continues, shame is firmly lodged in the person's life.  In every facet of a person's life, from the time they wake up until they return to sleep, shame is relentless.  It kills off the competition it finds in the human experience of joy.  Shame is one step short of suicide, emotionally and physically. It's the cancer of the human spirit.

Shame cannot be removed until a moment of truth is discovered. That moment comes with the ability to speak words like these: "I've been ashamed all my life, and I couldn't admit it." Or you might simply have the experience of a deep "knowing" that you've been deceived for a long time, and now it's time to see yourself in a new way. When a man stops denying shame, he can have first awareness that joy is a possibility in his life. He can make the hard choice that's necessary, in order to enjoy the full human experience.

## Making a Friend of Shame

Stepping out from under the shadow of shame is a process of affirmation, of reaching (or creating) that powerful moment when the unfamiliar whispering voice says "it's not too late to feel loved and wanted;" and you recognize your own voice as the whisperer.

The second step away from shame is making friends with it. This starts with embracing the truth that shame has been a part of your life, and will probably continue to be a part of your life. The key is to understand that shame isn't all that you're capable of feeling. You need to know that shame will continue to come up for you, and it doesn't have to be the experience that stops all other emotion. You might learn to ask yourself, "What would I be feeling if it weren't shame?" By looking at other possible responses, you can give yourself the gift of seeing yourself as others can see you. This is a step in the direction of compassion for yourself. Compassion is part of acceptance, and this can become acceptance of the man who is on the road out of shame. That's the moment when you might begin to affirm the value of your own life. That's when you choose emotional life over emotional death.

Because you can begin to value your life, you'll feel the increase of your value in the lives of others; and this is further affirmation that your life truly matters. This is the path out of shame, and it can't be walked in isolation. I have to recommend that you choose a qualified psychotherapist as your guide in this, because this isn't a job for amateurs. The person who is qualified to help you on this step is a person who can accept you unconditionally as the man you are, without judgments, and with awareness of the need to affirm your existence as you are, as a man in a process of profound change.

Shame is so effective at creating isolation that it's extraordinarily rare for a man to move out of shame without a helper. Only by creating the experience of having been witnessed in full human emotion can a man move beyond shame, because he has no experience of his work being affirmed by another. This is what enables a man to diminish shame's hold on him.

## Author's Note

Originally, this section started out by saying "The subject of shame is so large and so important that we can't possibly do full justice to the subject in the space that we can provide for it." This statement stopped me cold in my tracks, until I recognized it for what it is. It was shame, and I'm willing to name it, so that I can move on, and bring you the value that I know I can bring you. Shame's a killer. Don't let it kill you.

Finally, I want to say that I'm also grateful that so many valuable contributions have already been made to the understanding of shame, and that I'm blessed to know a man that I consider to be one of the principal contributors in this area. For your next reading on this subject, I urge you to see *Men Healing Shame, An Anthology* and *Breaking the Shackles, Bringing Joy Into Our Lives*, both by Dr. Roy U. Schenk and Dr. John Everingham, as Editors. Shame is a huge and important subject in the lives of men. The joy that many of us can take for granted is almost totally unavailable for men in shame, and awareness of the suffering they endure is necessary if we are ever to understand the struggles that men face in this time.

# Chapter 11
# A Blessing on Your Journey

In my mind, I can see you standing right here, in front of me. This is a really hard trip you're about to take, and you can do it as long as you know that you can ask for help. Asking for help comes from a place of humility, and from knowing that you may not have everything you need for doing something alone. That's a lesson that can't be taught; you'll learn it as you go. And when you've learned it you'll know that even when you're at the hardest place in the road, all you'll have to do is ask, and you can do whatever needs to be done, as long as you know that help is available.

You also need to know that there are going to be pitfalls and curves and turns in this path that are going to be confusing and frightening. You're going to be unsure about where that next step is supposed to be, and there will be times when you won't know the next step until you have to take it. You're going to have to keep going, even though you're not sure where that path is taking you. Trusting in yourself will take you to that next step, whatever it may be.

Something I want you to know is that you're going to be afraid. Men that have taken this journey of self-awareness have told me that the thing they need most to do is almost always the thing they are most afraid of doing. Their fear tells them that the thing they fear most is the thing they have to do. So, listen to your body, and if you find fear in the place where fear shows up in your body, take that as a sign that it may be your body's way of telling you that something has to be done.

You've always been on this journey, and at times you've carried such heavy burdens. So, it's time to let you know that the journey doesn't have to be so filled with heavy burdens. Maybe you've lived your life up to now with the feeling that you had no good choices to make. This journey will be a place in which you can make choices, and you will need to make choices. It can be a journey in which each moment is a moment of joy, simply because you can choose to let each choice be a source of joy.

This is just the beginning. The journey will always be incomplete, because you'll always want more. You are enough as you are. Can you step into the serenity you can create, and enjoy it? One of my favorite blessings invites a man to take a minute, and look inside, and realize that he has everything he needs, if he just connects with it all, to be perfect in everything he does, and he just recognizes the beauty and the power that's inside.

So, it's time. Go on your way, Brother, your journey isn't done. And there's always more joy, just around the next corner.

# Additional Reading

The places that scare you: A guide to fearlessness in difficult times-Pema Chodron

When things fall apart: Heart advice for difficult times- Pema Chodron

The Courage to raise good men- Olga Silverstein

I don't want to talk about- The legacy of moral depression- Terrance Real

The way of the Peaceful Warrior- Christopher R. Conty/ John Less

Transforming Anger: The HeartMath Solution for Letting Go of Rage, Frustration and Irritation- Doc Childre and Deborah Rozman, PH.D.

Homecoming: Reclaiming & Championing your inner Child-John E. Bradshaw

Breaking Free of the Co-dependency trip- B. Weinhold, J. B. Wienhold, Forwarded by John Bradshaw

Bradshaw on the Family: A revolutionary Way of Self Discovery-John E. Bradshaw

Healing The Shame that Binds You- John Bradshaw

Taking Charge of ADHD; The complete Authoritative Guide to Parents – Russel A. Barkley

A bird's Eye View of Life with ADD & ADHD: Advice from Young Survivors- Chris A. Zeigler Dendy, Alex Zeigler

The Seat of the Soul- (1989) Gary Zukav

The Drama of the Gifted Child (1997) Alice Miller

Fear The Fear And Do it Anyway (1988) Susan Jeffers,Ph.D.

Breaking The Shackles,Bringing Joy Into Our Lives (2005) Roy U. Schenk and John Everingham

Further Along The Road Less Traveled (1993) M. Scott Peck, M.D.

Conversations with God . an Uncommon Dialogue (1997) Neale Donald Walsch

Alcoholics Anonymous, 3rd ed. (1976) New York:AA World Services

Sexaholics Anonymous (1989) World Services, Inc.

Sex and Love Addicts Anonymous(1986) Fellowship-Wide Services, Inc.

Men and the Wound (1985) (Audiotape) St. Paul, MN55107 [524 Orleans St., (612)291-2652] :Ally Press.

Iron John (1990) Robert Bly

A little book on the Human Shadow (1988 ) Robert Bly

# About the Author

Alberto Minzer was born in Montevideo, Uruguay, and lived the first ten years of his life there. He speaks fluent Spanish. Alberto is a talented, accomplished, and experienced psychotherapist. He is passionate about his work in assisting the healing of others. He's helped hundreds of individuals, couples, and families learn to live healthy, productive, and meaningful lives. His direct approach quickly and effectively helps others heal themselves. "It's what you choose to do with your emotional and psychological baggage and pain that determines your healing. Pain is inevitable; emotional suffering is optional."

His writings about interpersonal relationships have affected many, and includes published poetry. He writes in the same way that he provides therapy, with compassion and awareness of what he feels in his heart about the human struggle.

Alberto has his undergraduate and graduate degrees from Loyola University of Chicago. He is licensed in the State of Illinois as a Licensed Clinical Social Worker. He pursued additional training in addictions, and is certified to intervene in this area. He has independently practiced since 1983, and has worked in diverse clinical, mental-health settings in the public and private sectors. He consults to Fortune 500 companies and provides Critical Incident Stress debriefing workshops and consultations. He has functioned in administrative and clinical supervisory capacities, including supervision of master-level therapists of psychology and students in clinical social work.

Alberto's commitment to personal healing led him to be actively involved in men's work with the Mankind Project International. He participates in men's personal work in both English and Spanish-language trainings throughout the United States.

As this book goes to press, a translation of this book in the Spanish language is beginning.

Made in the USA
Charleston, SC
26 December 2010